# Who's Talking?

## The Search for Who I am

# Rudolph Unt

# WHO'S TALKING

## The Search for Who I am

### Published by

Copyright © Rudolph Unt 2012

Front cover photograph of Rudolph Unt at 4 years old

Back cover photograph of Rudolph Unt by Pete Doughty

ISBN 978-0-9571733-0-9

*'The birth and death of a million thoughts fell from the stars and the One that could see and hear said, 'Why did you make me think! My stillness and silence has changed. I can see the world now! I will begin to walk it until I die. What is death? Is that life?'*

# Who's Talking?

## The Search for Who I am

# Contents

# FOREWORD

This book is a journey into finding our Spirit. The book begins as a man who is cynical and abusive slowly evolving through a winding road of questioning in honest awareness. In that process the God of Judgement is removed as we grow in our awakened consciousness revealing the beautiful Holy Spirits that we all are.

I am taking you on a journey along this twisting road of human experience to a place that you will know and recognise as a calling within you. This book is simple and rough and at the same time complex and profound but by the end you will know who is talking.

It is a journey into knowing your Eternal Spirit and the end of suffering.

This book will constantly challenge your beliefs of how you perceive your world leading you on a Soul journey into the awakening and recognition of your Holy Spirit.

The book was written in times of great upheaval and difficult change showing my shifting emotions as my indomitable Spirit forever shines through and becomes the witness of my eternal calling of Truth and Freedom born in Love's embrace.

# CHAPTER 1

# THE CALLING

I have found the Truth of who I am and what the human Spirit truly is.

What gives me the right to talk of the Truth?

How do I know the Truth?

In my life I have been and I have lived many characters.

I have been the loser and I have been the winner.

I have had money and I have been penniless.

I have been the priest and the devil worshipper.

I have laughed until my sides have burst and I have cried the deepest sadness to the point of death.

I have brought life into the world and I have taken life.

I have chased false love and opened my heart in the deepest love.

I have danced under the stars and the moon and toiled in the grime of factories.

I have challenged politicians and priests.

I have been the light of the party and the loneliest person in the world.

I have held birth in my hands and death in my hands.

I have been the liar and the truth teller.

I have been the judge and the guilty.

I have caused pain and suffering to the ones I love and I have given joy and love with an open heart to the ones I love.

I have been as clever as the greatest minds and as thick as a brick.

I have failed more than I have ever succeeded.

I have believed in God and I have proven God does not exist.

I have had broken bones and broken others bones.

I have been the drunk and the teetotaller.

I have lived with the best and lived with the poorest.

I have been the boss and the servant.

I have had fear that has gripped me for years and have had joy that has wiped away the fear and the tears.

I have brothers and sisters and I have friends and enemies.

I have been absolutely right and absolutely wrong.

I have been a thief and the giver.

I have been physically strong and on death's bed.

I have been the hero and fighter and the oppressed victim.

I have been the artist and the poet and I have scorned them both.

I have been the magician and the Spiritualist.

I have been married and I have been divorced.

I have been one with creation and one with my Spirit but mostly separate in Mind's dream.

I have been the rebel and I have been the conformist.

I have drunk with princes and with rogues.

I have followed my Heart and I have followed my Mind.

I have taken total responsibility for what I have done and I have run away from my responsibilities in helplessness.

I have been the follower of others and I have stopped dead in my tracks not knowing which way to go.

I have been a healer and I have been a soldier.

I understand the magnificent creation of the universe and I have believed the soaps to be true.

I have run free but I have always come back to my habits.

I have cried for the suffering of the world and I have cried for my own suffering in selfish indulgence.

I have parachuted out of planes and dived in the depths of the sea, sat on the desert sands and the rainy outcrops of grey mountains.

I have danced around the sacred fires as a shaman and sat on a park bench watching the world go by.

I have been a child and I have been a man.

I have empathised with the tears of others with true compassion and I have judged others with a cold heart.

I have blamed the world for what it has done to me and I have blamed myself for what I have done to me and I have released and forgiven both.

And I am still here.

But in all of this I am still searching. But for what?

Every one of us, no matter what we do with our lives, we know that there is something missing. That is why the majority of us live half lived lives looking for anything to fill that missing something and then ending up feeling exhausted and tired by being defined by our suffering in not finding true happiness in our desires.

But the truth is, I am still here, knowing deep inside there is this 'Forever' feeling that I am something else.

So who am I then? Ultimately I am not looking to find 'Who' I am. I want to know 'What' I am.

I have heard people say,

*'You are love and light.'*

What rubbish is that? If another 'goody two shoes' tells me I am 'love and light' I think I will batter them because I know they are lying dogs! And how do I know? I know because I used to be one of them.

I heard somebody say,

*'You are Oneness having the opportunity to experience individuality.'*

What on earth is 'Oneness'? I know in theory we are all 'One' but my mind says, 'That is too boring to even contemplate.'

I heard,

'*We fell from the stars to shine in God's loving embrace.*' Well he sure didn't embrace me!

It has been said,

'*The only truth is you are the awakened God.*' I would like to believe that but it does not pay my bills. I know the quick answer is, 'Yes God does,' but I can't believe that pious crud.

I also heard,

'*You are life's longing to be free,*' but really we are all imprisoned by the dream of freedom, never actually embracing it because there is an illusionary price on freedom.

I heard somebody say,

'*The creator of love is the Spirit, the enemy of love is the Mind. Only in Spirit to Spirit can we truly love.*' Just more bloody excuses to take us away from our sad pathetic half lived lives!

I also read some real deep stuff the other day,

'*I am the Eternal Truth not felt by Mind.*

*I am beautiful questioned by Mind.*

*I am a free Spirit imprisoned by Mind.*

*I am Love and Joy pretended by Mind.*

*I am a magnificent radiant light of life controlled by the dimmer switch of Mind.*

*I am silent witness to all creation overshadowed by the fear of death of the Mind.*

*I am Love awakened rocked to sleep in Mind's dream.*

*I am Oneness which Mind always points to but never can see or go there.*

*I am the Holy Spirit in God's embrace.'*

Blimey! That sounds like the, *'Conversations with God'* stuff! I will need a few beers to get my head round that one or maybe go for a run!

## ANGELS

Jumping the gun though, the other day some 'goody two shoes' was giving me the Angel rubbish. All that stuff about how we have guardian Angels that protect us and save us from our sad pointless lives. So, I decided to recontemplate Angels.

I don't think I believe in Angels in the way the world paints them but I did see an Angel the other day. There is a dear old lady friend of mine who is a Spiritual healer. As I was driving down the road an old man had collapsed on the pavement and I could hear the sound of the ambulance coming.

There was a crowd gathered around him and one lady was holding his head in despair like he had died and the rest stood around like second class mourners. Then I saw this friend of mine, this lady who is a healer. She pushed the people aside, took over from the woman who was holding him and put her own hands upon his head, with no words said, from what I could see. She is a very beautiful healer and I know her work. She was only there for a short while as I was in the traffic jam, then she quietly got up and melted back into the crowd and moved on. Moments later the man lifted up his head and was awake. This was an Angel doing its work. She is the only Angel I know, an unrecognised light amongst the people and a silent worker of God's Angelic touch and prayer.

I think, getting a little deep, that every one of us is an Angel not knowing that just with a kind, loving, gentle touch we can heal others. We are all fallen Angels who have just forgotten that every one of us once had wings. But what the hell do I know? I am just a regular dude in a hard world. Not really. Still got a whole pile of cynicism left in me.

## JUMPING MIND

As I was thinking this, my mind has jumped again. Always this jump of mind. ADHD problem I guess? Can't hold a thought for long!

Maybe it's because I get bored rigid with the blah blah blah stories that I hear every day from people hauling their baggage around with them like they have some crazed monkey on their backs, all trying to justify why they struggle in this unforgiving, selfish, cruel journey called Life, which I have been pretty good at myself. Anyway we all suffer from ADHD. See how often your thoughts change and jump? It just depends on how long it takes.

A woman was once telling me how awful her life was with eyes full of tears. What she was telling me was that her husband hates her, she hates her husband, her son is in trouble with the police, her daughter is hanging out with an addict and she is asking me, 'Why is God punishing me?' And I felt like saying, 'Because he doesn't like you!' Of course I didn't say that! I was just thinking, 'Why ask me with my track record as a loser?' Really she is just crying to feel loved and feel safe in a situation she can't fix and her husband and her children are doing the same.

All I could tell her is that her head is so packed with thoughts and worry there is no room left for anything else to come in. Everything she sees happening around her in her life is only a reflection of the fears and turmoil within herself. What you think of others is only a mirror of what you are within. You can only ever experience what you are within yourself. The strange thing is that what you think you are, is not who you are. If you let your fears go just for a moment then there will be room for peace where you can feel and see glimmers of who you truly are?

WHERE IS THE TRUTH?

You may be thinking 'Well where is the Truth?' Well follow me and I will take you there through this journey of being and seeing. I know what you are thinking,

'Am I interested in the Truth?

Do I care about the Truth?

Do I really want to know the Truth?

How do I find the Truth? Maybe the Truth in some magical way will help me find happiness, freedom and control over my stressful, sorrowful, unfulfilled and safely mediocre pretended life,' which usually just means getting through the next day with the least suffering as possible. If you are one of those who have everything you are really thinking how much better you can fake yesterday's bullshit with a pretended smile of honesty and truth in your own personal form of conceit. Showing apathy between forced smiles with daggers in your eyes your actions appear so absurd and the many masks you wear are only pinned on by the nails of greed and your own hidden fears. Ouch! Did that hurt?

Oh my God! There is my mind drifting again pretending to care about all this stuff but actually I am just sitting here looking out of the window on a beautiful autumn blue sky evening, just jumping around with thoughts until I grab one that has some feeling or meaning which in it gives a message.

Oh, and by the way, if you are one of those literary perfectionists where everything has to be grammatically correct in a perfect story, well this is my story and how I say it! And I know swearing is only what the inarticulate ignorant uninformed do in their uneducated minds!

So OK maybe I am some sort of subhuman!?

I am writing this book because I am as mad as hell, like Jesus turning the moneylender's tables over in the temple. This is not anger. This is Spiritual frustration breaking the shackles of the Mind's lie!

Suddenly echoing in my mind's ear I can hear a friend of mine. She is a lovely lady who has probably done every Spiritual course under the sun and she has suffered in the most awful way which I don't need to mention. She was shouting out 'love and light' but not one word of it was said from the heart, only in Mind's cleverness claiming the truth.

Strangely this might sound like I am bitter and twisted but the truth is I have never been bitter and twisted in my life. I have tried to be but then I know it is all a lie because it is only in Mind's control that we become that way. Actually as far back as I can remember I have just known that I am here. Some beautiful presence within me that is always here but never seen. This was her saying words in pretence of saying, 'I am in control and I understand the Truth,' but said without any conviction or faith like tossing a coin into a beggar's hat.

## REAL MAGIC

One day a young man came to me for a reading. He was dressed in black leathers and had long black hair and extra black eyebrows, a mixture between a Goth and an EMO, with pentacles hanging off him and various rings and jewellery on.

When he sat down he said to me, 'I am Witch and I have got all this power. I can make people do things just with my thoughts. People are scared of me because I have this power. I can do spells and conjure up demons. At night time I can fly and levitate off the floor.'

So I said to him, 'Well if you can do all that then why do you need to come to me for a reading?'

He answered, 'Because I hear you are into Witchcraft and stuff yourself and I don't know how to curb this power, how to deal with it or how to harness it for good.'

I just said, 'Is that true? Do you really have this power?'

'Yes,' he said.

So I answered him, 'OK I want you to prove it to me. Look at that tarot card in front of you and make it levitate and then I will know you have got the power. And don't do it by magician's means, by magic tricks, because I know them all.'

'Ok,' he said.

So there he was with his hands stretched out making noises, humming noises, distorting his face, staring at the cards, glaring with such focus and after a minute or two he stopped. And I said, 'Well the card didn't levitate.'

He answered, 'I am feeling a bit weak today. I had a big argument with my girlfriend.'

'That shouldn't make any difference,' I said to him, 'you have either got the power or you haven't.' So then I said, being cruel, 'You are just dreaming to have some kind of amazing power so people will think you are special, in your need to be appreciated and loved. You are even wearing the kit to look pretty convincing.' Then I added, 'I have got the power. I can make things levitate. I am going to levitate the card in front of you to prove I am more powerful than you. Watch this. This is real magic.'

I picked up the card, held it between my fingers and put it back down. Then I said to him, 'That is real levitation. I have the power.'

And he said 'No you don't, you didn't do anything!'

So I replied, 'Yes I did. Let me explain to you. Imagine God or consciousness in the beginning of time forming the universe and creating this world, this beautiful Earth with its vast oceans. Then the same consciousness formed life upon the Earth and created human form and filled it full of its Spirit, this invisible energy which animates the physical form to look and touch. This invisible force within moves my hand to pick up the card and put it back down. That is real magic.'

Then I did the magic trick where I hold the card between my hands and pull my hands apart and the card levitated in front of him.

He then jumped up and ran out of the room saying, 'I knew you were a bloody Witch!'

I just couldn't help myself. Well after all, I am a Magician too!

## SOUL AND SPIRIT

When the words Soul or Spirit are looked up in the dictionary they both say basically the same thing. In the Oxford English Dictionary the Soul is described as '*The immaterial part of man regarded as immortal or as animating the body.*' and the Spirit is described as '*Separable from and animating the body.*' Both are very similar.

So what are you? Soul or Spirit? Both function from within your physical form. As things can get confusing with many different uses of the same words this is my understanding from thirty years pursuing and working in many different Spiritual arenas and also from what I have observed within myself. It dawned on me we are both Soul and Spirit, not one or the other, and by knowing that it was like a brilliant light shining on a hidden secret scroll which unravels the confusion of man's conflict in trying to find purpose and reason for existence in duality.

Who you believe yourself to be right now, and who you think you are, is your Soul persona formed from your Mind not from your Spirit. Your Spirit within you is what you are in actual truth.

We dance our Soul personality creating emotional memory and forever building our identity in the drama of the Mind's story. That feels great but that is not who we are. When you die what is remembered of you is your Soul personality, or Soul person, which was formed from fear based belief that you became through your living experience. The moment you die that is the end of your Soul personality, the end of your story and the end of your belief but you are remembered by everyone around you as that Soul personality whether you were good or bad.

You are identified by your Soul personality formed from Mind's judgement which then becomes your story and the drama of your life with all its Mind's emotions that creates this Soul personality who you think you are and everybody else thinks that is who you are too.

Your Soul and your Spirit are two totally different things but living through your physical form. It is only your Soul personality which dies with its physical form but your Omnipresent Spirit, which can never die, is always taintless, timeless and innocent. The Spirit that you are is eternal forever. Your Mind and Body can only live through your Spirit but can never be your Spirit. Your Spirit is your true self, your consciousness manifest as a Spirit being. It doesn't pursue intellect and it doesn't pursue love because it created both of those things and is both of those things. It pursues creation and manifestation of creation. It speaks via your intuition and your instinctual feelings. The Soul personality is like a wall hiding your true beautiful Spirit that you are. It is for you to become pure Spirit personality with its own unique expression in the Oneness of consciousness living your daily life.

Blimey I didn't even need any tinfoil on my head to write that!

## SPIRIT

I see the God within us as pure consciousness, the Source of all creation, the life force that permeates all existence and we are that Oneness having the opportunity to fully experience individuality. I see our unique Spirits, upon the death of the physical body, going back into that Source of life, the Oneness.

The Universal Consciousness remembers our experiences and every event that ever happens, because it IS all things. I feel we leave signatures of experience in the tapestry or web of the consciousness of the universe as individualised Spirits in human form.

We are all sparks of the Divine Will and our Spirits are needed for creation to unfold. Everything has a purpose. We are like atoms that make up the blood cells in the life force of God without which God could not be. We are children of consciousness co-creating with God. Heaven is the bliss of being totally connected to the Oneness which is eternal and Omnipresent. We are God and God is us.

We are Awakened Love. We are already the perfection we seek to find. Creation is formed from Love. That love is without question. Love has no attachment. Its power is Spiritual freedom, only giving of itself so that consciousness can form different aspects of itself not wasting one second in manifestation.

We are Spiritual beings having a human experience. We are the truth living and feeling life. The only way you can ever connect absolutely to your Spirit is to surrender to stillness, to the nothing, in which is everything. This is beyond words and thought.

The Spirit world is not separate from us. We are the Spirit world. We are eternal beings with never ending possibilities to experience and grow in the Universal Conscious. The Spirit is the ultimate expression of God and creation. That is why Spirit is eternal.

There my mind goes again!

IS THERE A HEAVEN?

A lady came to me the other day and said to me, 'I want to talk to my husband,' and 'Is there a heaven?'

As you know I am a psychic medium but seen by the world as a fortune teller, a cheap psychiatrist and a pretender of powers.

I answered, 'No you can't talk to your husband. He is not in heaven.'

God did her face drop! You know how you get days when you just want to be bitch for the fun of it!

Well I calculated I have done over 25,000 readings or more over the years and you get to know human nature deeply and profoundly and the human story with all its patterns. There are some days when I just know they sit in front of me wanting me to answer a question and they will never believe my answer anyway or take it seriously. And why should they? So the occasional honest slap makes them open their eyes and look up at me in shock. In that moment we have eye contact and then they can see through my bright smiling eyes there is a Spirit world, just for a second. It doesn't matter how grown up we become we are forever children suckling off the words from the breast of ego's dream.

What I mean is her head was asking a question without any form of engagement, just looking past my shoulders, repeating some cathartic dream that maybe the man in front of her could prove and show her some mystical magical effect that would lighten up her heart to see and listen. When she saw my eyes, when our eyes met, she knew there is Spirit. No other words were needed.

Sitting within us is the kingdom of Heaven. Living within us is Heaven's kingdom. I just thought I would share that with you.

## NON-DUALITY

All this moving and jumping from one thought to another is like sticking flags in the ground on a pathway to somewhere. Like a silent pulling and calling to a place only my heart knows and sees beyond the veil, that which can be felt but can't be seen or held in Mind's thoughts.

The other day I went to one of these non-duality meetings where the speaker was one of those beautiful people who have let go of Mind's duality and become One. Is this non-duality true or just one of those new clever ways to erase the suffering of your life and Mind's experience just by letting it all go, past and future? I can see that but there is one thing that gets up my nose, even though I have experienced it myself, and it is when they break out into this 'Oneness' laughter in a smugness of Spirituality. I was sitting there thinking, 'I can take all this stuff but don't you bloody dare break into pious laughter!' I too am life's longing, or should I say, letting God live through me. I know it is innocent laughter but, if I am honest, it kind of reeks of not being quite true making my Spirit react like there is something missing but the real lesson was that the man behind me said to the guru, 'I can't let go of who I think I am even though I know it is not me.'

And the guru was basically saying, 'You have to and then you can giggle like me.'

Suddenly I was inspired to say to this man, 'It's OK to have a personality. That is the dance of life. Just don't take it seriously because we are all One anyway.'

Not bad from a dude just sitting at the side and not quite sure of the truth.

FINDING ONENESS

We are told that the way to finding Oneness in non-duality is by getting rid of our false personality and stopping all Mind's thoughts which will make you One with all things in awareness which is nice but doesn't really work because that in itself is a duality.

What I would like to say is that by letting go of your identity, or your Mind's persona, you reveal another you; Oneness that has an individualised personality that is vast but is not made up or created through the

Mind. If you follow the process of non-duality removing all identity you will find you do not exist and there is no centre to you, which is true. And when you sit in that place it is vast and beautiful and the loving heart of God shines from that point. This leaves you in a strange place because you are no longer wanting or desiring anything of the Mind so you just sit there doing nothing because you don't need anything.

So how can that relate to the rest of humanity and how we live our daily lives? This then lets your Mind jump back in and say, 'That was a great experience. Done that,' and then it is thrown into your goody bag of Spirituality. Then you are back into your duality world feeling lost because something has changed in you and you know deep inside that this world isn't what it appears to be once you have tasted Spiritual freedom. It becomes too complex as the conceptual world pulls you left and right. This is why a lot of people give up because they missed the one thing that is staring them in the face.

Think of this statement,

*'We are Oneness having the opportunity to experience individuality.'*

**The real personality that you become, that reveals itself, that walks upon this Earth, is a person that**

**is individualised as Oneness and rejoices in knowing that truth.** Christ and Buddha and any other enlightened being were that absolutely! In that you have the Oneness persona that walks the Earth that is aware and intelligent, awakened honesty and truth. This can make you feel isolated in the same way as your Mind will always make you feel separate and alone but it certainly feels more peaceful and loving. I don't want anyone to become isolated or feel isolated because they have woken up to, or felt, the Oneness that they are which then makes them clearly see the Mind's world as endless suffering, shackling and imprisoning. Because they can't change this they feel lost and alone and when they do talk to others of such things no one seems to understand what the hell they are talking about.

In this process you are emotionally constantly moving between the Angel and Devil within yourself making you feel disempowered. Slowly this disempowerment works upon your Spiritual courage by twisting the truth within you which can easily let you fall back into Mind's dreams for it is less painful than observing the insanity of the world.

What will be revealed as you go through the book, even though you may not understand it right now, is that you are more beautiful and vast than you can ever possibly imagine. Even more vast than non-duality. I feel that the purpose of creation is to find the realisation that you are individualised Spirit formed from Oneness, or should I say consciousness, which then in turn makes your consciousness individualised and in that individuality is your uniqueness as Oneness living, experiencing and expressing itself as a vast shining light of God.

Blimey! I just realised I need to get my washing out the machine so I can get it dried. Sorry, was I being serious for a minute? Don't think that by being One you get out of doing your washing! I don't want anyone to think I'm some kind of ivory towered elitist giving you some new shiny smug philosophy. I am human just like you wanting to know what's real. This is not something you throw into your Spiritual shopping basket.

We created duality so we can live our Oneness! It is our dream imagination that gives us purpose to exist. It is in Satsang we share association with living loving truth! That just popped into my head because God popped in to my head.

# CHAPTER 2

# TRUTH

What is all this Truth malarkey about then? I think we are all just habituated bullshitters anyway if we are honest! What does the Truth look like or feel like?

The Truth in the world is the acceptance of the uninformed herd's repeated beliefs accepted by the many that then becomes our Truth on some twisted moral ground. Money and power dictate morality and we live and die by that Truth even though we know in our hearts that it's a lie. If we are honest none of us knows what the Truth is in the conceptualised Mind. It is just an idea enforced by repeated physical behaviour. You can't make a Truth of the Truth and if anyone says to you, 'I have found The Truth,' somewhere, however they colour the story up, they are lying dogs!

Maybe the Truth is a hidden secret that can never be found? Or is it just simply because it is always here because you are always here? Truth is only found through honesty. When we are honest in our Spirit then Truth will come and sit with us and hold our hand and show us the way to freedom and freedom will open the door to the light and stillness, to your heart of love, in the revealing of the absolute Truth of our Spirit.

Maybe the word Truth is not the right word because the word 'Truth' is so fragmented in the conceptual Mind which in itself can never put a finger on what Truth really is. Truth is an energy which is boundless and spacious, that reaches out to the corners of the universe, that heals and frees all human suffering and is only ever looked upon and felt when silent honesty sits within us in the present moment. Honesty is the witness of Truth and the doorway to let it pour in. Honesty is Truth speaking. Not right and wrong. The word 'Truth' only has a dual meaning in Mind's eyes. Truth in Spirit is a silent witness of all creation. Some of the voices of Truth are kindness, compassion and peace. They all release the invisible Truth which also gives power to courage and freedom of Spirit and absolute awareness showing that consciousness, or you can call it Spirit, is alive in absolutely everything. Everything is alive. The Truth is that nothing ever dies. Death is the movement of silent Truth. Whatever the silent Truth moves through is the death of the Mind's fabricated lies. The emotional fear of death is only born in the fabricated lies of the Mind where the emotional God of judgement is born.

## STRING THEORY

Our Spirit is the God within us feeling the endless energetic energy of Oneness divided in the duality Mind. This can only be felt by Spirit but never understood by Mind. Judgement, love, courage, truth, honesty, compassion and fear are just some of the energetic states that we as manifesting Spirits can experience emotionally in our humanness in the movement of God's consciousness.

Consciousness and energetic energy is string theory in action. We have many words that express energetic energy. Vastness and simplicity run on the same timeline and both make you smile.

Maybe we are here to evolve to ultimately say to consciousness, 'That is enough,' even breaking God's dreams.

Did you ever get to the end of Angry Birds? What just happened? Did I just flip to the B side!? Did I ever say I was normal?!

## HONEST TRUTH

The honest Truth will change your life. The moment you are holding Truth within you your perception of your home, family, career and patterns will change. You will change in a good way because in Truth the lie that we live, or should I say the falsehoods of our beliefs of how we live our lives, will shine out to you like a beacon of pretended identity. When Truth enters you your world around you will appear to be different because it is seen through Love's eyes.

Many of you will find that your family, friends and community will suddenly reject you or think you have lost the plot. A lot of people who find the honest Truth within them will find that their old life will never be the same ever again. And even if you want to go back to it you can't because you will know that you are only pretending.

Many people who find the absolute Truth within them, that silent witness, lose everything. They can lose their relationships, their jobs and their homes. They can end up left with nothing at all and that is a very scary place to be. When the beckoning Mind jumps in and says you can go back to that place, as long as you follow the herd and keep your head down, you will find that even though you have lost everything there is a fire within you which just says, 'I can't go back. I don't even know why but I know I can't go back.' It is only when you get to that point that you begin to build a congruent life which is not easy because there are no books or teachers telling you how to do it. It has to come through your Spirit.

The biggest danger in this place is you have to catch yourself because your Mind claims everything, even your sense of truth and freedom, because it is always the first voice that talks from within you Your Mind is that voice in your head which becomes your words which you live your life by.

The Truth can only be known within you but can never be affirmed by anyone outside of you because it is only your pure heart that knows the Truth that you are. Truth can never be found, only felt in the still and silent witness of our honest pure feelings. If you only sense it for a second then in that lonely place there are a trillion Angels looking at you with loving hearts and big joyous smiles on their faces. So don't be afraid to go to that lonely place of honesty for it is full of light once you open the dark doors of your Mind. I only found this out when I realised even my issues had issues!

## EMOTIONAL SELF-HARM

We must not be afraid to feel and listen to the simple silence of Spirit, not Mind's false quietness. Your Mind keeps you as a spectator in your own life. The

Mind observes the world but also your Spirit witnesses everything in silent awareness. Wherever the perfection of Truth is felt Spirit enjoys the pleasure of it. When you become silent awareness walking you feel and see the solid vastness of eternity of the universe that runs through you.

Our Mind is like habituated self-harm. We would rather feel pain than feel nothing at all but in the nothing is everything you have ever wanted and then your Mind says, 'How can that be because it is nothing.' Your Mind will never know who you are because it empowers you and motivates you in fear and suffering.

Emotional self-harm is your resistance to the Truth of who you are. This self-harm is also known as your habituated addictions. It is our feeling of disappointment and being disheartened that this world is not as perfect as the perfection that we came from. We look at everyone thinking they are real and we are not and we would do anything to become real like them and let them give us our identity of who we think we should be so we are accepted into the gang and the herd world. How mad is that then? I say mad meaning causing Mutually Aided Destruction in the fear of separation.

When you wake up every day your Mind will start your day with habituated self-harm thoughts like,

'Oh my God I haven't got a job. Oh my God nobody loves me. Oh my God I am not as good as everyone else,' and when experienced there is a bizarre liking in that initial feeling of effortless suffering. There is almost a pleasure in suffering, just for a moment, and the rest becomes grey and dark in clouded depression.

## GOD IN THE SKY

Isn't it funny how we say, 'Oh my God,' first? But when we ask, 'Oh my God,' first, we are asking the God in the sky to find an answer instead of the God within us which always has the answer and sets us free. Can't you see I am just trying to put God back in you because he never left in the first place? When we put God in the sky we become separate, the perfect coup for the Mind to twist our heart of Love in the cruel excuses of the Mind justifying itself that separation is normality.

When God is in the sky we can blame God for everything and the same God of the Mind gets you to follow its truth as a servant that is not worthy unless it follows the so called moral commandments written by Mind's God in the first place. A God that doesn't even know who you are. The day we put God in the sky was the day we began to kill each other in fear and anger for we can never do that if we recognise

God within each other. Deep stuff eh? For don't we all live our lives in fear that we are separate from the world, from each other and from God in the sky. We have no chance when thinking such thoughts because they are fears that the Mind will use to affirm your identity in the Mind's world of greed, tradition and religion.

Can't you see that God is in you and also pours through every blade of grass, every tree, every animal, everything? And your Mind says that's not true because you are separate. Your Mind uses separation telling you in a profound way that you are alone and because you don't know who you are your Mind will tell you in judgement who you are. In feeling that you are separate and alone you are cradled and welcomed into our world of Fear.

# CHAPTER 3

# UNDERSTANDING FEAR

**Fear that causes separation from Spirit is the suffering of the world.** Fear walks hand in hand with judgement. I feel to say that 90% or more of the human race live in fear.

We have interpreted fear in so many ways and no one seems to have found the answer to what fear actually is. Fear is a real energy that resonates through thought. We have all evolved in fear based genetic survival which then is claimed by the emotional duality Mind that corrupts our experiences which then become part of the forming of our archetypal characters known as our Soul personality. Fear itself is a real energy that has been labelled by the Mind as need and desire. It is the number one motivational energy that motivates us to do things.

What I am trying to say is that virtually everything we do is fear based.

Some of you may think, 'My life isn't fear based because I do good things for good reasons.'

This is where you have got to be honest and look at the reasons you do things. Do they come from fear based belief or the feelings of honest truth of your Spirit? We have to look where fear comes from. First it comes from our animal instinct needing to survive which is hotwired into us. Then we have Mind's emotional fear which in itself gives us energy to motivate ourselves to do things, with thoughts such as, 'Better find a job or I will have nothing and if I have nothing then I am a failure. I have to be kind to everyone or they won't like me,' or 'I have to worry for everyone so they will be safe.'

## GREED, TRADITION AND RELIGION

How much of our life is fear based when observed? Think of greed, tradition and religion. Greed itself is fear needing to have more based on survival instinct. Religion is fear that if you don't do what God tells you to do then you are wicked. Religion is profoundly tied up with the fear of death.

Traditions, such as Remembrance Day, were created from the historic memory of the fearful destruction of humanity in the honouring and remembering of untold suffering of man's inhumanity to man. So in the fear that this may happen again the most powerful countries prepare for war to keep the peace but we can't kill more people to honour the dead.

Can you see from this that they all remind us that fear is always chasing us? So what is this fear? How do we get rid of it? Fear is the birthplace of emotional suffering. Fear motivates us from little simple fears to deeply embedded fears. For some women they have to put their lipstick and makeup on before they leave the house. In that is fear of not looking beautiful or of hiding how they feel about themselves. In non-fear based identity the woman in her pure loving femininity, her true self, would only paint her body to express how she feels good about herself not for the approval of others.

On a larger scale there are fears such as, 'This country will attack us so we had better attack them first.'

Fear is always motivational energy to do things, to get up and do stuff, for the majority of mankind. Even loving people can be fear, fear of not being thought of as a good person or caring about them or worrying for them. Remember fear isn't anger it is an energy.

There is fear love and there is love that just is. It is fearful love that ravages our relationships.

FEAR BASED INTENTION

We have to stop living our life from fear based intention and identity. The funny thing is we can't stop ourselves from doing this because our whole life has been the slow forming and building of our identities through fear and that fear itself makes us believe that we are separate beings and have to find life in the desires of fear. That is why any desire formed from fear is always short lived and empty because fear then fears losing what it feared to want. Shit sandwich eh?

Fear convinces us we have to pay a price to live. Fear is a debt you can never pay back. Fear is Mind's creation. Fear creates fear. Fear creates identity. Fear creates purpose. Fear proves you live. Fear motivates you to do things. Your Spirit has not been created out of fear for it is always here. This is who you are. Only the body that identifies itself in fear dies with suffering.

The funny thing is we fear letting go of fear for how else would we identify ourselves or motivate ourselves because we can't see or believe there is anything else other than living through our fear identity. By the way the 'other' is your Spirit, the

Forever manifest within you but because the Mind can't see you or believe you exist there is only Mind's duality fear that proves your existence.

The reason why we can't let go of fear based existence is because we don't believe we have a Holy Spirit. The word 'holy' means being whole, full of God's grace. That is why when we are tired and have had enough of the fear of our lives and struggling and surviving and we just stop and give up we feel lost and empty. We don't know what to do because our fear identity is all we have ever known and so we wait for some external new story built on fear that pushes forward or down to death. We only appear to identify ourselves through fear and fear itself convinces us that there is nothing else. But did you know the times in your life when you feel truly joyous and happy some other energy was motivating you without fear - your Spirit.

## THE FEAR DANCE

Fear is the birthplace of our addictions and hidden secrets. How do we catch ourselves and ask questions to recognise what things we do and what thoughts we have are fear based and what stories we create are fear based and motivate us into doing to protect us from fear so fulfilling a never ending circle of suffering? It is in catching this understanding that you realise that this is not who you are.

We have danced the fear dance for so long in our life's journey that there is a point we come to where we say, 'I am fed up with this and there is something missing in my life,' like a magical shift into looking into the unknown without fear. Fear is separation reinforcing itself in emotional stories in a million complexities of emotional identity which becomes who we think we are and we will go to any length to reinforce that on a daily basis.

Fear is what happens in separation when consciousness becomes individualised consciousness. When this is misunderstood fear becomes the fertile ground for human suffering not the beautiful experience of individuality.

We fear letting go of fear into the greatness and wonderment of what we are because fear itself can never understand this magnificent Spirit and we fear letting go of fear itself because we don't believe we are Holy Spirit but the moment we do Mind's fear dies forever.

Spirit is living fearless. We are taught to create from fear. We are taught to identify ourselves through fear. It is remembering that fear isn't fear it is an energy which the Mind has taken to point you away from recognising your Spirit that gave the Mind life. We are taught fear on top of our instinctive fear. Fear is the shackles of death's calling and Mind's power. It builds your houses and temples from the living to become tabernacles and mausoleums for the dead.

What is a church? Is it not anaesthetisation from the fear of death and cathedrals for the dead in fear's glory?

Religion will make you fear death and the same religion tells you that you won't have death if you follow this God in death. Fear will make you believe anything is real.

Did you know that anything that is built from Spirit and spoken from who you truly are is remembered and lives in your heart forever?

Emotional Mind's habituated fearful memory is not natural instinctive fear.

THE END OF WARS

If you can really get your mind round this it will set you free of every shackle that has ever held you not because it has been the enemy but because it has shackled and pushed your Spirit aside for so long that your Spirit says, 'That is enough. Time for freedom.'

Fear shapes us and imprisons us. People use it every day to break our Spirits so they can control us into becoming slaves of the Mind. It is used in families, religions and governments and is accepted as common world fear. The nuclear bomb doesn't keep the peace it holds us all in the fear of annihilation because we haven't understood and released the emotional energy of fear. For without that fear there would never be war or nuclear bombs. We created the nuclear bomb because we can't trust ourselves to let go of fear in Mind's dream. We use fear to keep the peace. Doesn't that say it all?

When humanity does not live in fear but is awake in Spirit we will build churches and buildings that all humans can be in awe of, built by the magnificent beautiful creative ability of free Spirits that honour the glory of what we can do from love based identity, even though any we build that shows the greatness of humanity are nothing compared to the tabernacle of the planet Earth which, when we open our eyes, shows us how beautiful we are in the physical temple of Spirits longing.

## TEMPLES OF HUMANITY

What I am saying is that the time will come when we let go of our fear based identities forever and the churches and tabernacles we build will be built on honouring the gloriousness of man's ability to build monuments that reflect all of humanities' greatness.

Everyone will be able to pass through or sit and look up in wonder at the amazing potential that we are and can build in the honouring of humanity without fear. But then we stand outside the temple and look upon the sunrise or sunset of the most beautiful inspiring temple that we ever made for us to wonder in – the Earth. Fear ravages the Earth and even ravages the temples of our bodies. It never honours them.

## FEAR BASED PURPOSE

Let us not kid ourselves that fear is the outside threat because everywhere we look is fear based purpose and motivation from within. That motivation can be doing something or giving you purpose to dysfunctionally destroy yourself. All fear leads to destruction. Look at the world. You are bombarded every day by fear. The news on the TV is fear based. The newspapers are fear based. Our societies are run on fear base. Religions are fear based. Our relationships with each other are fear based. We are so adapted to fear that we breed fear into our innocent children because the moral ground of fear says that is normal.

Let us not forget as well that the moral ground is built in our generation on money and power that uses fear as the yardstick for its moral ground. If you can see that from the day we have awareness we are born into a world that lives fear based and we learn to identify ourselves in that which then becomes our conditioned way of perceiving the world and creating our own identities of ourselves built on fear's perception. That is why the world is a mess.

When I say mess, I don't mean the natural world. Man's Mind is a mess and the mess of the Mind rapes and fills the Earth with the ugliness of pollution and polluted thoughts. I know this sounds grim but I am not here to give you bubbles of 'love and light' and bury the energy of fear that is ravaging you and our world.

The fear I talk of is not our natural survival instinctive fear but it is the fear that our duality Mind has claimed in its extreme emotional controlling in the forming of our false identities.

Fear makes us feel alive because it is an energetic energy.

WHO IS THE MASTER?

This section of the book is a biggy because without understanding this you will never be free or know your Spirit. Fear has always been a conceited justification of the Mind's ability to manipulate us into believing that our duality Mind is the master and saviour.

The Devil's tongue is spewing out fear based reality. When we feel lost and empty, unknowingly and unconsciously, we look back into fear to motivate us. This is extreme fear based manipulation so the Mind can control us and we become hotwired and habituated through almost every thought in fear based identity.

Our fear based lives and world hasn't got to be this way. There is an answer. There is a way to absolutely free us from this twisted warped emotional energy of Fear. It is when we just stop using it as our base of identity and purpose because the moment you stop doing that there is another person within you.

All the fear based worry has never changed one inch of your stature.

## WHO IS COUNSELLING WHO?

When we let go of fear, or just can't take anymore, we stop in shell shock; lost, broken and wounded. This can show itself in mental breakdown or depression. But don't worry we have got all kinds of pills to shove down your neck to fix that or even counsellors that sit with you while you tell them your fear story and how it has ravaged you. But haven't the counsellors themselves used the same conceited fear to give a false impression that they are in a position of awareness and neutrality as they tell you how to compartmentalise and manage your fears and send you out the door fixed for a fee? How can you ever be free or at peace with yourself in a fear based Mind?

Even Spiritual counsellors will fix your fears with some past life karma debt, or preordained negative template causing your rubbish, in their hidden fearful attempt to be in control and feed their own need to be admired or loved by giving you short term fixes. There are very few counsellors and healers who, in their hearts, come from a place of natural honesty who intuitively know the truth.

## THE EQUATION OF LIFE

We cannot ever understand the purpose of humanity or its conditions if we don't bring our Spirits into the equation. It is like the missing part of the formula which we have been searching for in the mathematical calculation that makes string theory work. When we do Spirit fills in the gaps where the fearful Mind has removed the truth. The day we remove Spirit we live in fear and confusion. The day we accept our Spirit, fear and confusion stops writing the rules and the history books and man's inhumanity to man. We can never change or find our true being and purpose without Spirit completing the equation of life.

Fear will always keep you as the observer of your life. You can't have Spiritual fear based purpose because your Spirit does not know what emotional fear is.

## FEAR IN RELATIONSHIPS

I am going to tell you a story to show how emotional fear and fear based identity motivates us into actions born from fear and ultimately keeps us imprisoned becoming our hidden secrets in the search of finding the love that we are naturally.

There was an academically intelligent woman who was arguing with her estranged husband. When he came to collect his daughter for the weekend she said to him, 'You are always late.'

He said, 'I am never late. I have only ever been late once in all these years when my car broke down.'

So then she says, 'That's what you think!'

So he answered her saying, 'That's the truth I have always been punctual. It is you that can't get out of bed in the morning! I know because I lived with you. I got up every day, took my daughter to school and even made you a cup of tea before you woke up.'

So then she said, 'If your daughter only knew what a loser you are.'

He replied, 'What do you mean by that?'

She said, 'You never provided for us.'

So he said to her, 'Well how come in all the years we were together I ran a business, worked every day and provided the best I could for the family? So at what point did I not provide?'

Her answer to that was, 'Well you were never here to do the jobs around the house or here for me.'

He said, 'Well duh, I was at work!'

Her answer to him was, 'You are always so arrogant and selfish!'

Which then made him raise his voice and say, 'You are not right in the head! That's why I divorced you.'

And at the same time the daughter was listening to all of this wanting to throw a bucket of water over both of them. Let's stop there.

Even in this little snippet everything that is happening is in their fear based identities, hiding their hidden hurts which are their fears manifesting and being reinvented in both of them. This is a no win situation. It is an emotional explosion affecting all around them, even themselves.

When I say emotional explosion I mean fear's emotional story. The man could not understand why after all this time she is still picking fault with him, pressing his buttons and causing a reaction. And he noticed if he didn't react to her she would work on the daughter and upset her and then he would be protective and come back to square one and be in an argument with her. He could not understand why even now she continued doing this when their relationship was over and they should be having a new healthier relationship. After that situation had passed he could not work out why when he was no longer rocking the boat and doing his reactive bit to cause problems. Then the penny dropped.

## FEEDING THE FEAR BEAST

She needs to feed the hurt and angry fearful identity that has been her hidden fears since childhood so it can reinforce and maintain its story. She uses the energy of angry emotional reaction to feed the beast of fear within her.

If he shouts at her then that energy feeds the beast that relishes in her victimhood identity. If he didn't react and walked away then she would turn to her friends and allies and tell them what a git or monster her ex-husband is and what a victim she is. Then they would get angry about how he treated her and that same anger energy would also feed her fear based personal identity.

Fear's food is negative emotional energy because all of us identify ourselves in fear which is the emotional fear whose master and father is the God of judgement.

I know what you might be thinking if you are a woman reading this - the majority of men are dickheads! And this bloke here writing the book is just trying to vindicate himself and cover up some similar story that has happened in his own life.

Let's look at his emotional fear beast.

When she is slagging him off in untruths he gets angry because he doesn't want to be seen as a failure. He gets angry because he got love wrong, because we can only feel fear which is born in us as children. He was disempowered as a child into believing he would never be good enough and because of his insecurities he would react to any false criticism of anything he believed not to be true about himself in his fear based story. That's why I say we all suffer even the children who are learning how to suffer from observing fear based lies presented to them in family arguments.

Remember the fear beast within you isn't who you are. The woman or the man. The fear beast was born from a fear based world.

## DEMONS AND THOUGHT FORMS

Sometimes we call these fear beasts demons. Why do you think we get possessed by demons? How many demons do you have dancing in you and pulling your strings? Sometimes we call them thought forms that are energetic energies that manifest themselves either short term or long term. Why do you think Jesus cast out demons and told people to sin no more? Sin is that fear that becomes suffering. So what is your fear based story that you live and die for? Fear is the suffering beast whose hunger can never be filled. If you can see that then you are planting the seed of Spiritual freedom within you, which is a brave thing to do, in your Spirit's honesty, not right and wrong honesty.

## CATCH YOURSELF IN FEAR

Now that you can see this you say to yourself, 'Oh my God! I can see how deeply embedded and programmed I have become and the whole world is lost and run by emotional fear too.' A world emotionally identified in fear turning itself into this immense energetic power that appears to be, and is, our motivating purpose.

Let's just catch ourselves. You might think, 'I understand that conceptually,' but really you are still absolutely hotwired sitting in your fear based personality and life because all you have ever known is your emotional fear driven Mind. Even this very moment it is taking you over again. Catch yourself and feel it. It's making you drop these pearls of truth in the grey mud of fear. Then again you fall asleep into Mind's dreams.

You can be free of this by asking yourself, with conviction of Spirit, 'Who's talking?' Is it your fear Mind or free Spirit? I have mentioned the word 'fear' probably a hundred times because metaphorically I am throwing these rotten tomatoes of fear at you. How many do I have to throw before you decide to step out the way because you have had enough? And my arm is getting tired with throwing them!

Vindication, arrogance, humiliation, Mind's desire, destruction and fear are all justifications of the truth in the personal conceited Mind of judgement. These build the feeling that this is the core of your being in which you identify yourself in fear and suffering because only your Mind has a core. Your Spirit doesn't have a core to identify itself from. When you release your Mind core persona your true self reveals its identity in Oneness and true freedom.

LIVING WITHOUT FEAR

Everyone holds within them the natural ability and the tools to live without fear but we rarely ever get the chance to use them. **Living without fear can only be done when we are aware of our Spirit within us** and we have become aware of how the fearful judgement Mind, through emotion, runs our world and lives. It is having the ability to discern between a fear based thought that creates identity or a fearless Spiritual thought that give you freedom in Spiritual identity.

You will never be free of fear and suffering unless you live your life centred and aware in your living Holy Spirit. That is your Holy Spirit free of Mind's control. Your fearless Spirit is Oneness experiencing individuality. Mind takes individuality and turns it into fearful separation in the sense of aloneness which is the birth of fear.

Spirit is aware that it is Oneness, which is individualised but not separate, in its longing to live and experience living life not separate Mind fearing life.

SNOWFLAKES OF SPIRIT

Like snowflakes, there are billions of us falling from the sky blanketing the Earth in life's longing to be. There is not one snowflake that is exactly the same as another but at no point does the snowflake think it is alone and separate. It knows it is unique in its personal expression of God's consciousness where fear does not exist. That is your living fearless Spirit. Snowflakes are made from water which come from the ocean of consciousness and life's longing to be. Frozen into snowflakes they fall upon the Earth like dormant miracles waiting to melt giving birth to all life in our Garden of Eden.

## THE CLOTHES THAT WE WEAR

Bringing this to a human level of understanding here is an example of the difference between fear choices and Spirit choices.

A fear Mind choice would go something like this. A woman might think, 'I need to go and buy a new dress. One that will make me look beautiful and attractive. One that will make my friends jealous of me because I have found something they don't have and it's the latest fashion. A dress that will hide my bumps and hangy out bits. And I even need to take someone with me to get their approval that my choice is the right choice, once I have convinced them, even though that person has no sense of dress themselves.' That is Minds choice.

Your honest Spirit's choice would be like this, 'I would like a new dress that I feel alive in, that shows the light that I am within and reflects my personality. One I feel comfortable in, that makes me feel good and shows my femininity not my vanity.'

Being fearless is enjoying the expression of your Spirit through your form and enjoying the form that you have that senses the world which it lives in.

When you live in your Spirit it does not really matter what you wear as long as you are happy in what you are wearing because it is the light of your being that shines out through anything you wear. When you are in the energy of your Spirit you could wear a hessian sack and you would look good. It doesn't matter if you are skinny or fat because the clothes that you wear will dance to your energy.

Spirit doesn't have a point of reference of fear. It transforms and adorns whatever you wear in love, negating any identity of adorning yourself in ego's fashion.

Being positive is the same as adorning yourself with clothes. Are they Spiritual clothes or fear based clothes? Being positive is fear based and anything desired from that ends up in suffering because it identifies itself in past and future beliefs of what would make you feel happy. Being fearless is only felt and experienced in the present moment in the expression of your Spirit wanting to create expression of itself not experience of itself.

# CHAPTER 4

# THE THIEF

We are all thieves. Our Mind is a thief. I can see that when I stop desiring. It is when we desire of the Mind that we become thieves. However we justify our actions we are thieves.

If I practice desire I suffer. Desire is the thief's passion which then becomes our prison, desiring more and hiding the fears of the Mind all wrapped in the habituated codependent need for survival, sex and relationships.

How can you tell the perfect thief not to steal? That's what it is. Your Mind is the perfect thief but innocently not knowing that it is a thief.

Your Mind will use any means to get what it wants or thinks it wants. It will lie and twist, justify and judge, pretend and create any story to acquire and if it can't acquire it will steal from you and tell you that you are the loser and the failure. The Mind ultimately is robbing itself. It is so perfect. All its belief is a trap leaving you feeling something is missing because the thief is on an adventure of desire and acquirement through physical form.

If you are honest, when you sit still and stop thinking and look back on your life and into the future, you realise everything you have ever done has been wanting, whether through survival, sex or relationships, leaving a wake of confusion and untruth.

Oh and the thief in you is the greatest storyteller of all. It will gently cradle you into a soft sleep and at the same time empty your heart and your pockets like an invisible jackal or laughing hyena both scavengers of the living until you are dead in a bizarre pleasure of desire. All Mind's desires give us short term feel good fixes and then we get bored and want a bigger fix because we love the pursuit of the feel good factor but, like our thoughts, we get bored of them.

The thief lies habitually in the Mind's dream. The thief is so good it will adorn people with gifts and presents and false love in the setup of stealing your very Spirit away into the Alcatraz prison of the Mind.

## SPIRITUALISM'S THIEF

It makes me think of when I was a little boy at the age of eight sitting in a Spiritual circle in a Spiritualist church with five old ladies, or so they seemed to me as a kid, only because I was told I could see Spirit, whatever that was. So I sat in the circle waiting to see Spirit with these old dears, actually more interested in playing soldiers with my toys once I got home. Anyway, I was there and in some mature way I thought I would listen and give it a go.

And suddenly one lady said, 'Look over there in the corner! I can see the Virgin Mary!'

Then her friend said, 'I can see her too!'

I looked and I couldn't see a thing.

And the lady said, 'It's very clear, can't you see her!'

So I looked even harder with all my mind reaching out, fixed on the corner, trying to feel and see but there was nothing. And I looked at the ladies' faces and they had such belief in their eyes I thought I was missing something.

Then another lady piped up with, 'I can see Jesus standing next to her!'

In that moment I thought, and if I could swear then I would have said, 'Holy Jesus! What the flip is going on? These are just five mad old biddies living in one-upmanship or some Spiritual bullshit dream.'

They had a gift of thieving any belief of the real Spirit world and, as a child and being honest by nature, I wasn't disappointed in myself because I did feel something. There was a greater presence there that they couldn't see and neither could I but I knew it was there. It filled the room.

Then as a child the ADHD kicked in and I needed to go.

As I left they said, 'Did you see her? Did you see Jesus?'

So I said, 'No,' and then I said, 'I saw God instead,' and that pleased them. Then I went home to play with my toys. I am saying all this because in the so called Spiritual arena there is a kind of strange game which so called mediums and psychics play which in reality is an emotional dishonesty to plaster over the weeping wounds of their sad pathetic lives. When you pretend identity in Spirit no one can really question you in case you are right and they are wrong. How ugly is that?

I best go and put the telly on and watch a soap and get filled with some other dramatised emotional bullshit. Is there a difference?

## BOARDING HOUSES

I guess you all need some point of reference so you can guess where I am coming from and leading to. My references are all of the colourful experiences I have lived through and observed and felt in my life's journey. They are all markers in time pointing to who I am.

Even though I was not fully aware at the time I knew something was unfolding within me into a person that I should be that has some divine purpose.

As a child I was open to seeing and feeling the energetic emotional reactions and visual multidimensional sensing of physical experiences. These formed invisible imprints in the innocent observer through a child's Spirit which became a template of my unaware future behaviour patterns turning me into the observer of human nature. Later in life I felt a sense of disheartenment in not seeing honest love in these people as they acted out their lives. Even then I knew that there was something missing, even in myself.

To put this in an understandable way, I grew up living in a house, well different houses over time, full of lodgers. My mom being the landlady of twenty boarding houses would fill every room, and every cupboard if you could get a bed in it, with someone living in it. I observed as a child every type of character from the gentle, quiet, sensitive Soul to the crazy madman with a knife in his hand threatening to kill people. Lodgers of all different descriptions from the lonely broken hearted to the doctor, the nurse, the priest, the racing car driver, the builder, the driver, the fireman, the policeman, the performer, the villain, the alcoholic, the drug addict, the whores and the wise ones.

I observed them all without any judgement for as a child I could not judge until I was told how to judge and what to judge. In my simple way in this house was all humanity including me. I guess this is where my intuitive free Spirit was formed and I began my quest of understanding humanness and ultimately dancing with the magical word, 'Why?' which in itself is the voice of God's longing to know himself.

In all the years that followed I never asked the question, 'Who am I?' I was too busy trying to find out, 'Why? 'and then, 'How?' But really, 'Why' is like the word 'perfection, it is a goal to be reached which doesn't exist.

FAITH IN DANGER

As a teenager I found faith in danger. Not insane danger but things like climbing 80' scaffolds just to see the view or climbing to the top of church roof tops just to see if I could.

I did martial arts to be the best fighter and fencing, Kung Fu and judo too. Being physical was something I could do which felt good. But in that I was one that could not do things by halves, it had to be to extremes. I had to be the best.

Even though I had no yardstick of knowing what the best was I just knew I had a physical aptitude for enjoying my Spirit within my physical body. This then leads me to another story.

My first job was working in an auto repair garage and shop as a shop assistant, cleaner and general dog's body. Being a wild Spirit I could not help myself from making fun of everything I did because even then people were being deadly serious about stuff. There are a lot of stories I could tell you about the things I got up to which would make you break your sides with laughter. It seemed, not really knowing at the time but I felt it, that the manageress of the shop and the men who worked in the garage did not like my youthful free Spirit. It wasn't as if I was a troublemaker or lazy because I would work from the moment I walked through the door to the moment I finished but they always used to give me the shitiest jobs like cleaning the top shelf that had not been cleaned for 20 years. I would do all they asked without question because I got paid. What was even more brilliant was I had some money of my own, even though it was peanuts in the scheme of things.

But then the day came when I was in the garage and the foreman came over and said to me, 'Rudi, I hear you do karate and martial arts.'

In my enthusiasm I had done karate since I was 10 years old and in my head at 16 I was Bruce Lee and I could do all the moves.

Then he said the dangerous words, 'Martial Arts are a pile of shit.'

Well guess what next? We had a standoff. A free fight, not a physical hatred fight but a fun fight, a test of the ordinary bloke and the karate guy.

So there we were on the greasy garage floor sparring with him trying to get his punches on me. Well obviously I blocked every one and then I swooped him on the floor which escalated it because he was a 35 year old grown up man and I was a 16 year old punk.

To me he was just playing but then he decided to pick up a broom handle and say, 'What are you going to do if I come at you with one of these?'

So I got a broom handle too, he not knowing I am flipping Bruce Lee with this too! I knew the moves. I ate and lived my art. So again I smashed his broom stick in his hands and I did a controlled blow to his neck with my stick. It just wobbled enough to shock his neck and then I stopped. Then I was called back into the shop, finished my job and went home.

The next day when I got in the boss was there with this guy saying, 'You attacked a member of staff.'

The man I had the sparring match with was painting this amazing story of how I picked a fight with him. I said to them both, 'We were just playing around. If that was a real fight I would have kicked his arse to the ground.'

Anyway, it was the termination of my job from that day. When I left he could become master of his own world again and be the macho man to the manageress. I had just experienced the injustice of a liar. The man for the first time in his life had been shaken out of his belief system and it was too painful for him to perceive because it reflected his weaknesses. This was my first encounter with how the thief Mind took humiliation and turned it into a lie to cover their hidden secret.

Bruce Lee once said, *'Those who are unaware they are walking in darkness will never seek the light.'*

# CHAPTER 5

# ASCENSION

I have just finished a reading with a woman who was telling me all about Ascension and how it is the new way for humanity and how the world is going to be saved, which was nothing to do with what she really wanted to know about or what was truly happening in her life. She asked me, 'What do you think about ascension?'

So we will stop here and I will tell you, not what I said to her, but what I really know about ascension.

Long ago, in my early days of being a Spiritualist, I had some friends who worked in the Spiritualist churches. There was one lady in particular who had worked all the local Spiritualist churches for many years and was quite well known.

She said to me, 'Rudi, I have got a secret I want to let you in on.'

Then she began to tell me the story of Ascension. How the Ascended Masters were talking to humanity through psychics, mediums and the spiritually enlightened and helping people to see the truth and save the world.

So I joined her little group of 8-10 people in her little one bedroom flat and we met up once a week, week in and week out, meditating on Ascended Masters and becoming an open channel and it was all absolutely fascinating and empowering. To write of Ascension is a book in itself but this is just the short version of it.

I learnt all about St Germain, the man who can never die, and three other immortals from the Bible who walked the Earth, many other great Masters who were prophets upon the Earth who lived and died and who are now in their spaceships talking to humanity through their Minds, raising the vibration of humanity into a $5^{th}$ dimension and even Jesus who is $6^{th}$ dimension and known as Sananda in the Spirit world or Maitreya in the order of Melchizedek. I even had their pictures sat on my mantel piece because I was channelling them.

To me this was resurrection, the answer to this messed up world. And in this group being shown the way by this woman, as it turned out, I was one of the 144,000 star seed which made me feel even better! I could feel the vibration in my body and my Mind resonating with these higher consciousnesses. I would sit in the group and I would channel Sananda and Kuthumi and as I channelled I would say the right words that would just come through me,

'The world is in a desperate state.'

'Man's inhumanity to man.'

'Indigo children are our future.'

'If people are feeling lost and empty it is only their Spirit changing to this new frequency of who they really are.'

I felt it too. All these amazing words were pouring out of my mouth saying, 'Don't worry. We are going to ascend. We are going up in waves. You can be in the first wave.'

I believed it absolutely. It even resonated with all my past lives which brought me to this point of awakening. These were good times and it made all the conspiracy theories real. I desperately wanted to ascend. I could feel the ships above my head in space waiting. I could see the ships cloaked by the clouds in the sky. I could see the message in the crop circles.

This was my time to ascend, to fulfil my full potential and purpose as one of the 144,000. This was my divine destiny.

So I chose a week when I was going to ascend. I sat in my little bedroom on a chair, meditating, totally opened up, my whole body resonating and vibrating in this higher light and frequency surrounded by the Angelic presence of Angels and Masters. I actually let go of all that I am; my home, my family, all that I had ever known. It was time to vanish and to be transported up.

As every day went by in my isolation I was eating morsels of food, drinking water, sleeping for a while, maybe just a few hours and then getting back in the chair. Sitting there I felt my chakras resonating to the higher frequencies, my aura expanding, slowly dismantling my atomic form, the atoms and molecules of my body resonating. I am going!

This was absolute conviction. As Jesus said, '..*if you have faith as small as a mustard seed, you can say to this mountain, "Move from here to there" and it will move. Nothing will be impossible for you.*'

I was the absolute. On the final fifth day I sat in the chair One with myself and all things. Then there was a silence. Just me sitting on the chair. My belief and conviction was so absolute that at that moment I truly believed I could go and be and do anything. I could even believe I could astral project to the surface of Mars! But I was still here and actually, truly, I was only feeling an unwanting peace and silence within me, a stillness that isn't still. And then my Mind started telling me that maybe I had missed something because I had not ascended.

I reflected back over how enthusiastic I was about this in recent weeks and how totally sold I was in Mind's dream of Ascension. Even going to the Spiritualist churches on Sundays, while on the platform, I was mentioning Ascension (although not the word) telling everyone that everything was going to be alright. I was so enthusiastic. I didn't feel disappointed I just sat there numb with myself.

Then a few days later I was back in the Ascension group with a new found honesty of reality. In my Mind I went through the whole process I had been in. It was biblical resurrection soup, said in a different way, but it was the same thing. The penny dropped. This was brilliant American masterful marketing of the God and Jesus story to give people faith that their life wasn't so hopeless. The next time I was at the Ascension group, when the lady who ran it went off to make us tea, I noticed down the side of her settee she had all these books on Ascension which made me very curious. And then as I quickly flicked through the books I realised that what she had been talking about earlier in the evening, all that I had believed she was channelling from other worlds, was actually in the books.

When she came back from making the tea she began to tell us about who she really was, her star seed name in the spaceship (I think her star seed name was Ankara), where she was going to and how the spaceships were always there waiting at any moment to lift her up where she would be in her rightful place as a star seed.

What she did not know was that, while she was making the tea, I had read enough of her books and realised where she was actually getting her information from. Mystical my arse! Then I thought, 'Ah bless.' In her longing to find love and faith and truth she too had bought into the romantic Spiritual lie of salvation. She believed her madness. Well logically, what about the other 6 billion lost Souls on the planet who had the right to ascend too! All of us were just duped by Mind's dreams.

On reflection, as an intuitive psychic medium, when I sat in the group and she held my hand and said, 'Are you channelling now?' I could not make sense of this channelling even though being Spiritual myself I could feel the intelligence and consciousness of the universe around me.

Then she said, 'I have been told you are star seed.'

Straight away I was channelling the exact repeated words of 'love and light' you hear from Ascended Masters. I was channelling. But I wasn't really, I was just saying what they wanted to hear. It was almost as if I had to force the words out of my mouth to get the approval of the group because I was a star seed. That filled my Spiritual ego although, in truth, I knew it was not true but how could I go against the Ascended Masters?

And so I was looking at this lady in front of me telling me about her new found faith in Ascension, something that 15 years earlier I was happy to die for. But what could I say? I know I wanted to say 'Get a life, not a Spiritual death,' but I just told her, 'Keep pursuing it and see how it unfolds.'

Oh and by the way. If St Germain is immortal what the hell is he doing in the Spirit world? I won't even talk about the tin foil on your head stuff and the Violet Rays! This was actually written on the day (28th October 2011) when the first wave was due to ascend to the spaceships. And did they? No they are still writing on the forums! Do you get it? Can you feel something in you is saying, 'Yeah, that's right.' If not at this moment then you will by the end of the book. Trust me I am a fortune teller!

# CHAPTER 6

# ROOMS OF THE MIND

I have got to tell you this story. This is true!

I live in a wonderful place away from the madding crowd and the only way to get to my house is down a bumpy old track, with no road signs, which leads to a little back gate which is the only way into the garden and to my front door. So when people come to see me for consultations I usually prepare my space and make it sacred.

The people who come call me first because they usually get lost and I have to give them directions because there are no road names where I live. Anyway, this one morning, which in honesty has never happened to me before in all the 30 years of reading, was one of those lazy mornings when I didn't wake up until late. I was unshaven, dishevelled, drinking my cup of tea, sitting on the sofa watching the news in my boxer shorts and T shirt, as men do, and the house was untidy. Then I got a telephone call. Two women were actually walking down the track towards my house telling me they would be there in three minutes!

And I thought, 'How did I forget this appointment? Holy shit! What am I going to do?' I am supposed to be this squared away, in control, groomed, utterly focussed clairvoyant and here I am sitting in the chilled out untidy mess after having had my own private party the night before! Bloody Hell! How do I get round this one?

In my mind I thought that instead of coming across as a clean shaven, tidy, squared away, Spiritual counsellor this is the day I turn into the hippy, unshaven recluse, as mad as a fish but full of wisdom. Well, that was the best image I could muster up to justify me being totally out of sync! I managed to tidy up and shove things into cupboards and under cushions and look almost liveable. Luckily my reading room was looking fine, but I felt as psychic as a brick. I just wasn't in the mood or rather I was unprepared I should say.

Anyway these two women arrived and decided to sit together in the same reading, thank God, but it was clear they were both ball breakers. What I mean by that is they were not going to react or say a word.

They were the kind who say, 'You are the psychic you tell me.'

There was no room for light talk and banter. They were watching me and I didn't want anyone to look at me because I felt so scruffy and rubbish. All I could do was smile and fake the world is alright. How mad is that? My reputation as a spot on natural intuitive accurate reader and psychic was being put to the test and scrutinised by two perfectionists. Normally it does not bother me who is in front of me but today I was acting out the dishevelled recluse.

As I began to read for one of them, every so often I would say, 'Does that make sense what I am saying to you?'

She would always say, 'Kind of,' or 'Maybe. Tell me more.' She was not yet going to give an inch to my clairvoyant wisdom, even though I knew what I was saying was 100% right.

This woman was so imprisoned by her Mind's thoughts she only heard what she wanted to hear so that she controlled, or should I say hid, the real beauty that was within her as a woman. She was desperately looking at me to find the answer why she couldn't break free from her struggles and suffering and the only way she coped was to be in control of every aspect of her life with an iron fist of distrust.

So I just said, 'You know you are here for one reason only, because your life is empty and you don't know how to fill that space because you are too hurt. That is why you came to see a psychic eh? ' This broke the ice and made her laugh. So I just said, 'You are in the Beat Up Room girl. How can you ever find peace of mind while you are there?'

Then she suddenly broke down crying. The iron lady had taken off her cloak and showed her honest searching for answers.

So I began to say, 'This is where you are. This is where your friend is as well.'

What I find really frustrating at this point of being aware of who I really am, is that wherever I go I just see everyone is asleep in believing who they think they are. I know I too was once like that. It is as if everyone gets to a point where they just want to get through this cruel, loving, mad, passionate world not knowing really why or who they are. Even the question itself is impossible to answer.

Really what I am trying to say is that we are habitually, constantly living in our heads and in our thoughts we believe to be absolutely true. The Mind reinforces itself by using physical proof, judgements and facts that create the identity of who we think we are. But what if, just for a second, we got it wrong?

The moment you say that your Mind will again jump in and say, 'Got what wrong?' This is how the Mind claims every thought to its own justification.

My thoughts just shifted again. I want to say something else. I am bored to death trying to work it out, to do the right thing, be the right thing, have the right thing, to be right. Isn't that right Mind? But as I say that and think those words it is as if they are no longer a part of my thoughts and who I truly am.

The best way I can explain this is we are always asking the questions, 'Why is it that I don't have, or should have or haven't achieved or should have more?' Our Minds work in a strange way.

So I said to her, 'This is called the Beat Up Room.'

And she asked me, 'What is the Beat Up Room?'

So I said, 'Let me do my best to explain it to you.'

THE BEAT UP ROOM

It is a bit like you sitting at a table with yourself at one end and another double of you at the other end talking to yourself in this room of the Mind. But this is a very clever room because you are gently held by the hand and taken into this room which has a frosty glass door and the person that takes you by the hand and takes you through the door is the double of you.

77

The double shuts the door and turns the sign around and, seen from the other side, it reads, 'The Beat Up Room.'

(Actually the Beat Up Room has two doors. It has a door in and a door opposite which is a solid door with no sign but I will tell you more about that door later.)

Anyway, you sit down at the table and there are two big chairs and you are there looking at yourself, both the same person. Next to the double you are talking to there is a filing cabinet with words written on it that you can't really make out. So here you are facing yourself in the Beat Up Room. Your Beat Up Room. This is where your hidden secrets can be talked about.

As you sit facing yourself your double says to you, 'Who the hell do you think you are? You think you are good enough to be loved and have all the things you want like a perfect life, perfect home, perfect partner, perfect job and perfect relationships? How on earth do you think you are going to get that? Just look at you. Look at all that is wrong with you.'

And then the list starts coming out. This is wrong with you,

'You are overweight.'

'You are too skinny.'

'You are not loved.'

'Too old.'

'Too young,'

'Too rich.'

'Too poor.'

You are never enough. The list will go on with all the things that are wrong with you, how you failed, how other people failed you and how you didn't quite make the grade.

And then the double says, 'It is all true because I have the cabinet next to me. It is called the But cabinet.' And as you sit there in your worthlessness the double of you says, 'Don't worry. I have got the answer. It is not just your fault, it is their fault. These are the ones who have abused you and used you. The people out there are greedy and selfish, your partners only pretend to love you but they don't really. I am here because I am your best friend and I care about you and we are going to find answers. But first of all, we can't find answers until we know what is wrong with you and I am expert at fixing what is wrong with you.'

Then your double says to you, 'Why don't you just ask me a question and I will give you the answer. I know you have got lots to say to me.'

The first thing you say is, 'I am terrified of being alone and that no one will ever love me.'

Your double answers, 'You know why. Just look at yourself. Who is going to love you? You are not beautiful enough, you are not clever enough, you have failed, you have had a rubbish life and you didn't get your chances. How can anyone ever love you? And you know what I am saying is true because, look, I can go to the 'But' cabinet and get a file out for you.

The first one is, 'Look how you have failed in your relationships. I have the file here that shows you failed. This is the memorial proof. And then you were rubbish at school. I have another 'But' file and it says your parents never loved you anyway. What the 'But' really means is you are being a useless twit and you live your life as a coward. But it doesn't matter because we are going to fix it, even though it is going to take a long, long time. And don't forget I am always here for you to talk to in the Beat Up Room.'

Then the double carries on talking and says, 'This is the answer. What you have got to do is think about what you really desire and go for it. You have got to get positive, get fit and don't trust anyone. They are out to get you out there so fight for what is yours because I know you are smart really. So the first thing you have got to do is to think what you really desire and get positive about it.

Anyway, your time is up so you need to go. We can continue this another day but don't forget I am always here to talk to. I am your best friend and I really, truly care and love you.'

So you leave the Beat Up Room and go off back into your world. The Beat Up Room is your Mind. It is the hidden secret that you don't tell people about.

Isn't it strange how when you are out in normal life the moment you hear or feel anything that saddens you or makes you fearful or when you feel your suffering, this invisible hand holds you and takes you back through the door and into the Beat Up Room.

You sit down opposite the double of you and you start discussing what is wrong with you, because there is always something wrong. But did you know you have been in the Beat Up Room all of your life without even knowing it?

Then after a while, not knowing why, one day you will go to the Beat Up Room and you will say, 'That is enough. I am tired of beating myself up. I have blamed the world for all my problems and I have blamed myself for all my problems and yet I still end up sitting in the Beat Up Room with my Mind.'

Then you get smart and you say, 'Right. I am going to talk to myself in the Beat Up Room. I have realised it's not true.'

So there you are. You sit down again opposite yourself and the first thing your double says to you, as usual, is, 'Who the hell do you think you are? Do you think you are smarter than me?'

But now you have learnt about ego in your journey. You know this is just the ego talking to you but then your double says, 'I am not just your ego. I am you.'

So you answer yourself back and say, 'You are just a liar. This is rubbish. This is all just not true and I am going to leave the Beat Up Room and never come back because you are in my head and that is all you are.'

Then the double of you says, 'You have got me sussed. You realise that I am just a liar, but with good intention, and I understand now that you have realised I have had to put you through all of this so you could find yourself and be taught life's lessons. I knew this day would come when you would suss me out but now you know that I really am your friend.'

And as you sit there thinking, 'I am free of my Mind and my suffering,' your double is saying, 'Yes you are. This is called realisation and enlightenment but I have always been here for you.'

So as you sit there looking at the double of yourself you look across to the other door and you ask the double, 'What is through that door?'

The double answers, 'Nothing much. You understand now that you are free and you know that I am, like you, a part of finding the wisdom that you are and I am always your best friend.'

As you hear this from the double you still know that what sits in front of you is only your fears, a liar. But you say, 'I have got to see what is through the other door.'

So your double says, 'Ok my friend. Come with me.'

The double opens the door and you look in through the door and see a room that is endless. It is full of tables with more doubles of you, thousands of them, and you say, 'What on earth is that?'

And your double says, 'I didn't tell you that bit. That is your Higher Self which is the God in you, which is me too. We are your ego. We understand and didn't we all help you find this realisation, this new you.'

You are shocked for a moment in thinking, 'What is happening here?'

Then your double shuts the door and takes you by the hand and sits you down in the chair opposite and says, 'By the way, who the hell do you think you are? All those in there know the truth.' Then your double continues saying, 'They have got your criminal records on file of all your failings and your mistakes and they have all been stamped so you can't get a proper life or a proper job because you are on record now forever.

Ok let's just look at this new belief you have got. That is all it is but we will find the answers because even all of 'you' in the Higher Room loves you too.'

Then in the blink of an eye you find yourself outside the Beat Up Room feeling numb like you have been raped by Mind's judgement and factual proof and clever belief but with a strange desire to go back in the room just one more time to ask one more question and fight for one more case.

But then isn't it funny how in the Beat Up Room and in the higher Beat Up Room there was something missing. Your Spirit. Only your Mind can go into the Beat Up Room! You have your Higher Self, with impossible aspirations, and your Lower Self, with all your failings, and you are in the middle feeling tired, purposeless and lifeless just waiting to be eaten by the gribbly of the world. By the way, the gribbly of the world is your Mind and you are its food. The Beat Up Room turns into a shit sandwich which then turns you into a coward ready to be eaten by anyone!

## THE COUNCIL OF THE WISE

As a reader, or should I say intuitive counsellor, when I read for people, I hear the human story reflected through my own human story.

Today I did a reading for a lady who is very spiritually aware, a psychologist who is also very practical. She was telling me that no matter what she does, how she understands, cleverly analyses and departmentalises and puts into clarity her journey, she is still unhappy and the same shit just seems to keep on happening in her life.

She said, 'Even though I am an intelligent woman and I learn by my mistakes I can't break this sense of something missing. There is a sadness that sits within me.'

We talked about this, the causes, the how's, the why's and the when's and how her life is still the same struggle presented maybe in different dramas but it is the same story. It is like there is some hidden demon unknown to her that seems to put the block on things. We talked about the roller coaster, her highs and then the fall to her lows all the time and it doesn't matter how hard she tries to inspire herself, change herself, anaesthetise herself or rationalise herself it just won't go away.

I couldn't really give her an answer because in many ways I was thinking and feeling the same. I had just had one of those nights when I was in bed, deeply troubled by my story and suffering, my successes, my failures and by my understanding that even though here I am, highly aware, highly understanding, falling in and out of being awake, I had unknowingly, but must of knowingly, subconsciously left a wake of let down and hurt to people I love. What is this thing that won't let go? Like peeling an onion, layer after layer, until you think you have got to the end and then suddenly there is another layer. So I engage with all that I am. For me it is like my whole identity, all that I have been, all that I have known and experienced, even though thoroughly understood, even though feeling I am awake and in my honesty, I can't shake off this connection to the Beat Up Room of my Mind and the But cabinet. I have truly had enough. I don't want this life any more. How can I help others when I can't even help myself? Then I did the wise bit in my own Mind because all of this is coming from genuine real life suffering and real life happenings.

So here I go into the Mind's room again. But this is a different room and it has a table with twelve people around it. This is the Council of the Wise, all aspects of me. I have a kind person, a rebel person, a laughter person, a fixer person, the teacher, a bad person of me, a hard worker, a lazy person, a lover, the fool, the wise man and the parent. So here I am at the table and I ask my questions.

First I ask the fool around the table, 'How do I let go of this invisible thing that torments me because I can't see it only feel it?'

The fool says, 'Don't take life seriously.'

Then I ask the wise person, 'How can I be considerate in all things?'

He answers, 'That is just part of life's complexities.'

Then I ask the rebel person and he says, 'Ignore it, just go and do.'

Then I ask the kind person who says, 'We are all the beloved of God.'

I could go round these people all night looking for the answer in the Council of the Wise but they could not answer my questions.

Then the penny dropped. I said to them all, 'Today you are all sacked. You are not real. You are all archetypes of life's longing for identity. I am the Captain of my Soul,' and they vanished. Just for a moment, just before they vanished, they all changed into doubles of me.

## DON'T GO THERE

The answer of how to fix this came to me in the morning when I woke up trying to find an answer to this continued dialogue with suffering and who I am and what I should be and what I should have. Then it became very clear. All these things existed from my past history reinforcing future belief, so my Mind was in the past or in the future but where I wasn't was here.

Even at the start of the day our Minds take the unfinished business of yesterday's thoughts and fears which prepares us for the yardstick of how we deal with our day emotionally. I felt detached from the world and the only way I could be detached in the world was to live my life by living there in past or future identity.

The answer is, 'Stop thinking. Just don't go there.'

When I say, 'Don't go there,' it is because every single day all we ever do is reinvent yesterday by going there in our Minds and trying to sort out why the past has caused us to be who we think we are.

By going into the past we are going over what happened in situations that gave us suffering or joy which has become our truth but then we keep studying it and seeing if it was their fault or our fault. If it's their fault then I am right and I will hold that belief into my future wanting. If it was my fault then I was wrong and I take that into the future as my guilt and suffering, my secret to be hidden from the eyes of people.

Isn't this strange? When our Mind is in the past or the future trying to work out a problem with the same Mind that created it and none of them actually exist because they are in future time or past time.

Both are our endless suffering, going round and round and round and the only way to break free of this and find the truth that we are is just to stop. Don't go there. Then you will find yourself in a place where you actually feel happy and with a sense of freedom. If you don't stop going there then you will just continue your habituated negative patterns to fill the present moment. We are all looking into the past or the future for answers. How many thousands of times have you gone into your past story? As you are in it you are suffering and you have never found the answer so when I say, 'Don't go there,' it is not because you are forgetting or shutting it off. You have been there a thousand times and it has not fixed a thing.

When I say, 'Don't go into the future,' it is because it is the future of your worries and fears and wishes. They too are suffering because for every desire there is a fear of loss which is another form of suffering.

Don't project yourself years into the future or with the word hope (which really is the impossibility of reason.) You have been there a thousand times too and it has given you nothing.

So when I say, 'Don't go there,' it is not switching off from responsibility it is pulling the plug on irresponsibility and Mind's judgement. Just try it for an hour and you will feel free and your body and Mind will start to fill up naturally from your true inner self with honest desire from Spirit.

The big reason that I say, 'Don't go there,' is that I am saying, 'Stop going into your bloody Mind!' It leads you to suffering and leads you to everywhere but here. Your Mind habitually takes you into the past for that is its identity and into the future for that is its fear. Both are suffering and that is why it seems you can't stop this endless desire of wanting, having, controlling, fearing and all the rest of the stuff in judgement's realm.

When you don't go there that is redemption from your Soul personality into living in your eternal Spirit. This doesn't mean that you can't think of the past or the future, it just means you don't go there trying to solve the fearful illusionary story of Mind. Instead you observe it with awareness without judgement and then it has no more power over you or, should I say, your Mind is no longer running your life.

If you start worrying back on this habituated endless cycle of codependent thoughts then you have to catch yourself and say, 'Stop! I am going there again!'

It is just mindless suffering which reinforces the person that you think you are. The Mind keeps telling you, 'You have got to go there. You have got to sort it out.' The Mind is endlessly telling you to go there because if you don't then you are irresponsible.

It is really the Mind saying, 'I have got you by the throat and I am not letting you go! The more you try to break away the tighter I will squeeze you to pull you back!'

Your past and your future will pull you to your knees and turn you into the praying beggar of the decisions of judgement that will keep you there until you are dead. But there is something in you that will always pick you up and end this process of 'going there.' It is the fire of your Spirit and knowing no matter what is dished out the Mind can never destroy you. By letting go of future and past suffering you are honouring your Spirit and showing the world you are alive and an ambassador to truth.

When you serve singularity of Mind's desire you spiritually die. When you serve the God that is within you the real humanity that you are will open and fill you full of life being reborn free to serve your purpose.

Stop trying to fix things because it is the addiction of Mind's control and self-identity. Spiritually you do not need to be fixed because how can you fix what is not broken? Only the Mind is broken. The broken Mind is the root of all the sicknesses of our physical form which kills us slowly in its lie of energetic fear. The sickness is the illness that ages us and kills us. You will then become aware that what we are actually doing is letting the salesman of the Mind sell us anything we want to hear. All the time the Mind is slowly wearing us down, making us feel absolutely tired of being defined by our suffering. Not going there is a surrendering, not a giving in, but an acceptance that it is just the way it is. And the way it is stays in the place it was formed and identified. For the demon of suffering is only held together by the story of the Mind trying to create a false identity, a persona of who you think you are. By not going there this is the beginning of redemption into freeing your Spirit to its true potential. Are you feeling it yet?

We have this split personality in our Mind like the Angel and the Devil.

One part is saying to you, 'You know you should love that person. They are just right for you. They would be good for you.'

Then the other person in your Mind is saying, 'Don't go there. They can hurt you. You will suffer if you love them.'

This is the kind of daily dialogue we all have in our Minds every day whatever the subject. Approval and disapproval of right and wrong decisions based on all our memories and desires and fears of the future, like a never ending schizophrenia. That is why you can't go there to find your purpose in life. There is another person that stands back, that is intelligent and wise, that observes the insanity of the duality Mind that you identify yourself with. The other person that stands back observing this is your precious Spirit. The real you. The Eternal Truth.

# CHAPTER 7

# DEPENDENCY & ADDICTIONS

Don't kid yourself for a second. We all have many addictions which are built up from childhood and through our lives, addictions that habitually manifest themselves because of the hidden demons, or should I say hidden suffering of the fear of being exposed to our true feelings.

We are hiding the love that we dearly want for ourselves constantly because we are divided either in our heads or our hearts and we are either living in our heads and making decisions or we are living in our hearts and making decisions. We hardly ever have Mind and Heart working together. While the head and the heart are divided we live in our addictions and codependency from others. It all comes back to the inability of human beings not being fully congruent in Body, Mind and Spirit. We all live in a dysfunctional way between one or two of these at any one time.

I need to tell you a story to throw some light on addiction.

A lady came to me and wanted me to cure her of addiction to alcohol. She said, 'If you can fix my addiction, which no one else has ever fixed and I have been to everyone, then I will tell the whole world! The whole world will love you!'

Well that appealed to my ego! That would make me a God after all. Well at least I would think I am! A man of my calibre should have the answer!

In my usual electric jaw way I said, 'Yes I can fix that too. I can even fix it within four sessions! Forget all your AA and hypnosis rubbish. I have found the way!' Bloody Hell! Who's talking now?

And then I was suddenly there with a challenge. How do I fix addictions? So there I am throwing myself in the deep end as usual but only because of my ego and not having the ability to say, 'No, I can't fix that'.

Let's see how I work this one out then. I prayed to my Gods, I prayed to my Angels, I prayed to my Buddha, I prayed to my shoes and to the sky above. Guess what? Nothing came back. The only way I could find a cure or a way out was to truly look at my own addictions and how they affect me and are deeply embedded in my habituated subconscious.

I had to look at how we get addicted and how it gets fed and becomes a regular unconscious need.

## SMOKING

Years ago I used to smoke and I stopped myself from smoking in a most peculiar way. To all you smokers out there. You smoke when you are happy and you smoke when you are sad, you smoke to make space and time to think, you smoke in your private isolation, you smoke at regular moments of the day even when you are working in your job and you smoke on call of any emotional high or low. The cigarette is a celebration of time and control you have over something that doesn't question you. It is your cigarette. You go out the back with the other smokers and it is your space and your moment.

I was into roll ups then so part of the ritual was to prepare my cigarette. I would roll my bit of card torn off the Rizzla packet to shove in the end so I didn't make a dog end, preparing a moment of contemplation and letting go of thoughts. These were my social Plato moments, where I could think and chill out and just be. I finished making this white magic wand that gave me permission, just for a moment for myself and gave me a little bit more time of peace. God it was fun smoking!

When I was smoking with my gang outside the office, or the shop, we were all honest with each other. Like inmates in a prison we got to walk around the courtyard free of the restraints of the imposed regime. It's funny how in those five minutes in the courtyard or at the back door we shared a common humanity. We were all smoking away with people also addicted and by knowing that we found that we talked honestly to each other about our real concerns. Then suddenly the five minutes were up and we were back in the prison, back in the regime.

What is this nicotine rush we are supposedly addicted to? It made me think it is not a nicotine rush at all. It is something deeper. What it really is, is an accumulation of emotional, intellectual and physical factors. It is from a combination of these that the addiction is born.

The emotional pay off of addiction is social. When your friends smoke, or if you drink a glass of wine when you are out, it becomes a part of the magic around you. It becomes habituated because it is regular but really the addiction began from the first moment you took your first drag.

I was 18 when I first had a cigarette, just encouraged to have one because my friends smoked and I guess, like everyone, I just coughed and spluttered my way through the first cigarette. It wasn't too painful or disgusting but taking in this smoke was just something my body had not experienced before. Let's really look at what happened at that moment in time and how this so called nicotine craving begins. It is said that 60mg of pure nicotine will kill a 200lb man stone dead. That is how lethal nicotine is. It is a poison. So the moment you have a cigarette your body reacts violently, not just coughing the smoke out but violently because it is a poison which can kill you. There are also all the other chemicals in the cigarette and the burning chemicals to burn the tobacco which tars up your cilia hairs in your lungs which causes the infections and the cancers.

So basically this one little thing is happening. You are being poisoned. When your body has been poisoned it creates chemicals in the blood to fight the poison. The anti–cancer chemicals that your body creates are basically your body reacting to being poisoned and it is the rush of these fighting chemicals that is the high, your body actually fighting against the poisoning. Your Mind remembers your body's reaction to being poisoned. It says, 'This is what it feels like. This is what happens when I save you from being poisoned.'

That is the so called nicotine effect and the high is the rush of positive anti-cancer chemicals fighting it. So what is really happening is that once you start smoking it is usually at the same times - after breakfast, mid-morning, after lunch, dinner, tea or sex. Whenever you have a smoke it is usually when you are socially relaxing and it becomes a symbol in your Mind of almost a healing space.

It does not matter if you smoke 20 a day, once a week or once a month your Mind remembers that you are going to be poisoned so subconsciously and psychologically your body, before you have a cigarette, is preparing itself to be poisoned creating this so called nicotine craving effect. It is actually saying, 'I am ready for you now to have a cigarette.'

So it really is a defence mechanism of the body preparing itself to be poisoned that is the nicotine effect, it is not the nicotine giving you some sense of bliss.

The day came when I decided that I didn't want to smoke anymore. Like some people I tried to stop with New Year's resolutions, or by telling myself, 'It's killing me,' or 'It's too expensive,' and all the excuses and reasons why I should not smoke because anyway it is killing me and causes cancer. It is a bit bizarre really, like being on a battle field and saying it is the other guy that is going to get shot not me.

So how do we stop? We find that we can't stop this because we have habituated chemical patterns held by emotional experiences of the good or bad. That is why it is so hard just to stop.

So I thought, 'Well how can I beat this? I have tried the other ways and they all failed and I have gone back to smoking.'

How could I beat something that exists in a conflict of Mind, emotion and the physical? What I mean by that is the interconnection of those three things.

Emotionally it is my best friend and emotionally I get rejected because I smell of cigarettes and am not liked. Intellectually everybody else smokes and I want to be part of the group. It is good to be part of the gang and yet intellectually I know it kills me. It even says on the packet it causes serious illness and cancer. Physically, chemically it is poisoning me and my body chemically is creating chemicals, positive energy to beat it. All of these add up to their own story so how can I stop? There are just too many pulls. It is almost like it is a whole person or a friend in itself that shares your life but never says a word. So how do I stop then? How do I beat this?

I knew the moment I made a conflict in my Mind that I have to stop smoking because it is bad for me then I am in a conflict of things I can do. To get positive and fight it is an energy in itself. I am strong enough to fight it. I am stronger than the cigarette. Even when you are out with your friends and you make a statement, 'I don't smoke anymore,' then suddenly you are in conflict with them and no longer part of the gang. They will try to coax you back in with a glass of wine or the sharing of the peace pipe, the peace cigarette. Emotionally you want to have those sacred five minutes, those little moments, and all of it is a conflict.

The answer was simple for me. I just said to myself, 'I don't smoke any more. There is no reason why or not to. I just don't smoke,' and I knew once I was out with my friends I could not tell them I had stopped smoking. When I was with them and they offered me a cigarette I didn't say, 'I don't smoke,' I just said, 'I don't fancy one at the moment.' There was no conflict, no engagement.

And then there was the chemical. How do I fight the chemical bit, the preparation for being poisoned in my subconscious?

The answer was I would just jump up and down on the spot for 30 seconds which made me laugh, and made people around me laugh like I was weird, which broke the chemical imbalance in laughter.

That was how I stopped. I still fancied a fag occasionally but I just didn't go there. That is all you need to do. It is no more complex than that.

I would like you to think right now how many addictions you have from always needing a cuppa at a certain time or not being able to leave the house without your lippy on or the deeper stuff like being addicted to argument or even to being right, addicted to codependency, drink, drugs and rock'n'roll.

Your addiction is not the problem it is the habituated anaesthetisation of your hidden suffering.

## THE HIDDEN FIRE OF ADDICTION

On reflection one of the greatest things I noticed in my addiction, which would apply to any addiction, was the preparing and anticipating the moment to smoke. It was like getting excited about going out for the night to a party. It was the rolling of the fag prepared for the right time at tea break.

In those moments there is an energy of manifestation of a desire or should I say the word 'desire' by itself. In that is an energy which is the hidden fire of addiction. It is almost a pleasure to be engrossed in the story of preparing yourself.

Addiction sits in the place where your Mind is separate from your Heart but they both agree upon your emotional fear based story. In all its social and personal stories there is one for the Mind and one for the Heart. When they don't communicate honestly with each other there is an empty space where addiction thrives.

This is because both will agree, your head and your heart, on addiction. In addiction you can do something, you can do it physically and when it is repeated it becomes the truth, the fact and a part of your persona.

Everyone has addictions, many addictions, which accumulatively become our hidden secret of our fearful longing to feel loved and feel safe. Addiction anaesthetises us when we can't find that. To break the addiction is not to replace it with another addiction.

How mad is it when you speak to somebody, say an alcoholic, and say, 'Right we will stop you from drinking and you will never drink again. You will become a teetotaller.' Is being a teetotaller an addiction too? What you want is to drink only for those moments you feel like having a drink in a non-obsessive behaviour. I think they call it being balanced.

Let us really look at how we stop this, say an alcoholic, but you can apply this process to everything including alcohol, superiority or being a victim. Whatever addictive pattern you have addiction is compelled to do and the compelled energy is deeply embedded subconsciously.

Right. That is all the serious stuff talk. What I would like to say is something else. The more you become aware of who you are you realise that your Body and you Mind lives in the temple of your Spirit even though the Body and Mind are lesser temples in their own right. In the highest temple of Heaven there are many rooms. The time will come where you will not want to drink or smoke anyway or abuse yourself intellectually, emotionally or physically because your Spirit within does not desire any of those things. It is always the brightness and the love and the peace that you are that pushes through your addictions.

How do we fix it then? Don't worry! Dr Rudi has the answers with his magical potions and elixirs!

But very seriously, this is what you do. This is the dialogue you need to go through in questioning the addicted energetic belief itself directly which will ultimately guide you to the centre of your addiction that was born from false belief and in turn temporarily anesthetises you from your suffering in short term feel good escapism.

When you pick up a glass, if you are an alcoholic, at the regular time of the things you do, the alcohol, the drink, is your dummy, your soother, like a cigarette or even being superior or right.

So if you imagine that you are an alcoholic and you have got to have a drink, just as you hold your glass to your lips ask yourself this question,

'Who is drinking?'

Look at the glass and say it again repeatedly,

'Who is drinking?'

Your Mind will say, 'I am drinking of course. Me!'

Then you say again, 'Who is drinking? Who is drinking?'

And your Mind will say, 'Don't be ridiculous. I am drinking?'

And you say again, 'Who is drinking? Who is drinking?'

And your Mind says, 'Give me a moment. I will tell you who is drinking. I will tell you why I am drinking'

Then you say again, 'Who is drinking? Who is drinking?'

Then your Mind will say, 'You drink because you hurt.'

And you say again, 'Who is drinking? Who is drinking?'

Your Mind will say, 'I am taking you away to a better state to make you feel better. I am numbing you from your suffering for a while because I am your best friend.'

Then again, 'Who is drinking? Who is drinking?

And your Mind will keep coming back, 'I am the drinker.'

And you just keep saying, 'Who is drinking?' and after a while your Mind stops looking for reason or excuse and you say, 'Who is drinking?'

And your Mind will say, 'I am drinking. The Mind is drinking. I am the drunk.' (Yes it is your Mind that is the drunk not your Spirit, the person that you truly are.)

And then there is a silence and your Spirit says, 'I don't need a drink for I am already joy and peace. I am calm and free always.'

And your Spirit says, 'Who is drinking?'

And your Mind says, 'Me. The story is drinking.'

Then your Spirit knows, without a word, that your Spirit does not need a drink and only your story needs a drink. Your Mind, that believes itself to be true and who you are, needs a drink.

The moment you stop and just 'be' the glass and the drink has no purpose. In this strange way you question yourself, 'Who is drinking? Who is suffering? Who is afraid?'

You are not asking, 'Why?' or 'When?' You are asking 'Who?' And when you repeat yourself,

'Who is here?'

'Who is drinking?'

You will hear your Mind say, 'I am here.'

And you will say, 'Who is here?'

And your Mind will say, 'I am here. I am suffering. I am right.'

And you say, 'Who is here?' and the more and more you say that you can feel the threads, the story of the Mind, will pull away from you and you will see it as it is. The story is the conviction, the story, the belief generated by the emotional Mind.

Then you can go a bit higher,

'Who am I? Who am I?'

And your Mind will say again, 'I am this person that you think you are. I am my job. I am my relationship. I am all my desires.'

And you say again, 'Who am I?' over and over 'Who am I? '

And slowly the silent witness within lets you see that you are not who you think you are. It is just a story reinforced by physical doing. And in that silence you are always here. Your Spirit is here. Not wanting or giving. Just living and being forever. And then, Oh no! My Mind just took control again saying, 'Is that right? Are you sure? What if you are wrong? What if you are right?'

Your Mind says, 'Fight the world. Get the world. Get what you want. That is good for you,' and the same Mind says, 'But I am afraid. I am unsure. I can't upset people.'

Isn't it funny addiction is only formed from separateness? It is formed from feeling separate, feeling less than, or even better than, other humans.

Even though the addiction itself is a short lived experience, it belongs to you and it is your friend. Addiction by itself is a lonely place but when your addiction is shared with other addicts there is a calling of humanity, there is a strange love. When you are in a group of people who have the same addictions you suddenly realise that you are not alone, there is an honesty in it, there is a good feeling, there is a vulnerability of innocence opened up and shared with other Spirits who are just the same as you, all born innocent finally imprisoned by Mind. Addiction alone is the pressing and pushing down and burying of your true self called Spirit. How big your addiction is depends on how far you are removed from the love that you are and the love you lost and the love that never understood you and the love that should have set you free to be the love that you are.

Addiction is born from our need in wanting to feel happy however that wishes to manifest itself. Over time this becomes a habituated need as part of our identity. You might think that being right makes you feel happy, laughing makes you feel happy, being in love and admired makes you feel happy or having control over your life makes you feel happy. Just think of all the things that make you feel happy or the things you wish to pursue that will make you happy. It appears this process is our natural normal human condition but once we have reached or gained the thing that makes us feel happy we always want more because everyone needs it, and once tasted it becomes our daily need to have it again. We all like to be identified in the feeling of happiness and those things that make us feel good.

In time this becomes an addiction and part of our identity like a saviour from our troubles. Being happy is our natural state. Our Spirit is happiness always. It wants to align itself with the joy that it is not with the joy it can find. There is nothing wrong with wanting to be happy because that is wonderful. Only when it becomes an obsessed addiction does it twist you into the chaser of short term fixes. It is very important that you become aware of what is addicted behaviour and what is natural joy. The Mind is expert at fearing not being happy and will form happiness addictions in the belief it's made you happy. But it never tells you that it comes at a price. How mad is that?

# CHAPTER 8

# LOVE AND RELATIONSHIPS

What of love? Well I guess with my track record do I even dare talk about it?! Then again, when I say my track record, I have not had many relationships in my life and they have always been long and sustained. But the question is,

What of love?

What is this love?

This is the big question. This is the big thing that runs through everything because the basic desire of all human beings is just to feel loved and feel safe.

That is what we do it all for. Even though the word 'Love' itself has been so weakened and diluted it has almost becomes a joke.

Well, the way I am going to talk of love is what I know for sure within myself. We are all Love awakened in Mind's dream. That is what we are, but that doesn't mean anything unless we dance with the words of Love.

As a spiritual counsellor and professional clairvoyant I would honestly feel to say that 70% of my work as a reader is all about love and relationships and how we dance in that experience. After literally thousands and thousands of readings, and also having had a colourful life with relationships myself (the word colourful is obviously the hidden word for hell in relationships but also the greatest joys) this is a subject I could, like any human being, talk about for days but I will try to condense it down into a human story.

It is strange that every reading I do which involves relationships is also a reading for myself and an understanding for myself of what the hell is going on in this insane pursuit of love and being loved. I will come to a definitive answer of what Love is which will be said from my Spirit not from Mind.

EXPECTATION

Expectation is a relationship killer, humiliations best friend and the bars of imprisonment of your Spirit.

This bit is for the women! How often, if you are honest, have you had this massive expectation of your partner? Only if they did this and only if they did that then you would be happy and feel safe and loved by them. You just want them to be their True Self. But guess what? It never happens. They never fulfil your expectations and if they did there are a thousand more where they came from! And whose True Self is it anyway? How do you think people react who have expectation on their heads? They give you lip service so they won't lose your love which is only given honestly from you when all expectations are met. It is also a play for time as well. How mad is that?

Expectation is one of judgement's best mates. Expectation is only your fears of not feeling loved or feeling safe. This is you wearing the trousers for the man you want to love you because if he truly understands your expectation he would be there for you with such integrity that you would feel so loved and understood and safe you could open up to be the free loving woman that you are.

What part of expectation has any understanding of integrity? Integrity is never found through expectation. Expectation is the murderer of love in Mind's dream. It is just another form of judgement's control which imprisons both of you so you can never talk the truth to each other.

Expectation is cruel, cold and unloving and lives in separation

## YING AND YANG

OK. Let's take it from here. I could talk of a thousand reasons of repeated patterns in so called loving relationships. I have come to an understanding for men and women that what we don't understand about each other is who we truly are, what a man and a woman's true Spiritual purpose is. It is a bit like the ying/yang symbol both entwined but free.

What a woman is in Spirit is pure love and what a man is in Spirit is pure freedom. But the woman can't feel all of her love unless she is in the arms of someone who is free. And the man who is free cannot be free unless he holds love within his arms. Pretty deep stuff eh?

Here is the bizarre dance of love and relationships. You may have heard of the popular book, '*Men are from Mars, Women are from Venus.*' Well I feel it's not quite right. We are all love's longing to know itself.

Ok the best thing I can give you as answers to know what Love is, is to take you into stories, the stories I hear every day. The conflict men and women have with each other.

I will start with what love isn't. Any love you feel that causes you pain and suffering is not Love. It is conditional love crying out for the truth of Love.

I will give you an example of a reading, which is quite common. It applies mainly to women but men also have it in their own way. It is this insane disappointment of having been let down in love and relationships and how we use the experience of the hurt and let down of old relationships as the yard stick, or the spring board, from which we prepare ourselves for our next relationship which then usually is doomed to failure too. I can honestly say, in my own opinion, that 70%' maybe more, of relationships they are not in love but pursue the wanting of love through a bizarre tangle of desired wants and needs, all fragile upon the altar of Mind's expectation.

## REPEATED PATTERNS

To give you an example, there was a lady who used to come to me for readings for over twenty years. She was a regular and the first time she came to me was about the breakdown in her relationship. She told me how her partner, who she was married to, became boring, weak, couldn't think for himself and did not satisfy her. She said she could not trust him, he was argumentative and she just wanted out. At the time she had found someone else and he was waiting in the wings. Her husband didn't know about this, the poor sod, but he was already history. History unfolding in a way that he could not make sense of. Women are bloody experts at dissolving relationships!

Hmm, was that a tinge of embitterment from me? Or perhaps it is sympathy for the poor guy who doesn't know when he is bagged and dispatched?

When a woman has another man in her heart, or her Mind, basically she dumps her husband or partner, and sometimes her children, but more often she takes the children with her because the children are her unconditional love. All she does is get rid of the boring twit.

Anyway the new man is in her heart making her feel like she is needed and wanted and she decides to open her heart and pour her love out to him. A year or so after the husband had gone she was with the new guy but then suddenly it was over and she sat in front of me again with a new story.

She was asking me, 'Why do I always choose men who are dickheads? Why can't I trust them? Why don't they do what I want? Why do they always let me down?

Well, the next thing I know, within three months there is a new man in her life and she is telling me, 'This one is my Soul partner.'

I remember saying to her in the reading, 'I thought your husband was your Soul partner or the last guy was.'

She replied, 'No. This one really is my Soul partner.' Then she asked me, 'Don't you believe in Soul partners?'

So I just said, 'No. If you believe in Soul partners that means that they knew you before you came here and maybe shared past lives. Maybe in past lives you had many other Soul partners who loved you absolutely, so in a strange way in the Spirit world right now there could be thousands of Soul partners all waiting to meet with you again. Isn't that kind of weird?'

SPIRITS IN HARMONY

I don't believe in Soul partners. I believe in Spirits in harmony with each other. What I mean by that is I do believe that you can meet another human being who you are in love with in unsaid Spiritual deep profound loving connection and it is in this way

119

when in pure honest open love you become Soul partners. Not owned, not contracted but knowing for eternity that for a while, or even a lifetime in this life, you have truly shared absolute trust of Spirit and Oneness. In that is the perfect love, a love where the Mind has no place to corrupt or disempower.

This perfect love is what we yearn for deep inside and search for. The yearning is your Spirit calling for what it is which is pure Love.

MIND'S LOVE

The Mind is separate searching for a Love that it does not know. Mind's love is whored out, conceptualised, emotional desire, pretending and faking Love itself. The Mind has no concept, not even for a second, of what Love is but it will grab your feelings and turn them into an emotional story and present it to you on a plate saying, 'This is Love,' but really it is just another mouldy sandwich! In our childish wanting to dream and fall asleep in love's arms we buy and bite into it with some hope (which is the impossibility of reason) that it will flower into something that is true but it never does in Mind's faked emotional love.

And the same Mind looks at that and says, 'How did I get it wrong? I will fix it so let me try another way.

I will be in so much control that you will not make a mistake with love this time around.'

Can you see it is all just Mind stuff again?

All Mind's love is pretended empty desire which always falls on empty ground. Mind's love lies upon the altar naked in its pretended beauty and grace and wanting, waiting for you to sacrifice yourself and to sacrifice the real Love that you are in its pretended giving desire for fulfilment. It is not an altar of Love but a sacrificial slab where your heart gets stabbed through. Grim stuff eh? But who hasn't been on the slab yet?

Anyway back to the story. The third new guy was with her for six months or a year and then he's gone. She comes back to me with the same story, 'All men are the same. All my friends think so too. You just can't trust them.'

I said to her, 'So you have learnt that you can't trust men?

And she said, 'Yes. Will I ever find a man that I can trust? Can you give me an honest answer?'

So I answered her, 'Ok. Not a hope in hell if you believe those thoughts. All low level Mind's love makes you want to possess and hang onto the love that you think you have, which is nice but at the same time it binds you both, men and women. In that binding of Mind in low level love you kill, or should I say push away, the true love that might have been in the beginning. A short term fix for long term suffering. What did you build your love upon? Was it the rock of the Mind or the ocean of loving Spirit?

Running through all of this you have your unfinished business of childhood sadness given to you by your family, your community, your culture, your religion and your country. You can never find Love in that. Only by knowing your own Spirit do you find Love.

Real Love is not as exciting as Mind's love but in truth real Love is the open heart of God that is more deep and beautiful and never ending because it only exists in the Forever.

We are not born into this world looking for power, knowledge and control. We are born into this world looking for the Love that we are always which then gets lost in Mind's dream.

Understand that a man is Freedom and a woman is Love Spiritually. At the end of Freedom it turns into pure Love and the end of Love it turns into pure Freedom. They are both one and the same Spiritually but not in Mind's wanting.

Get your head round that one!

## WALLS OF DISTRUST

You see, when it comes to relationships, very few of us ever have one relationship from the time we leave school until the day we die. The majority of us have relationships that end and leave us hurt and suffering. So what happens is that every let down and hurt and disappointment and broken expectation becomes an emotional sandbag which we build up in front of us. Sandbags made of judgement and distrust and we build this for every relationship that comes and goes, hurt by hurt and let down by let down.

If you can imagine you have this solid wall in front of you 70% built and the last 30% is the open space which is the hope that someone will come into your life with such love it will knock down the rest of the wall but you are still looking over the top of the wall that protects the front of your body and your heart. We all become 70% ers!

This means that when I ask any man or any woman, 'Do you want love?'

They will say, 'Yes I am open to love. I want to love somebody. I want somebody to love me.'

But what they are really saying is, 'I am 70% shut down and sandbagged and won't let anyone in. They have got to prove that I am safe with them. They have got to prove undying love for me and then I will open my heart 100% and be happy with the right person.'

But the truth is you never get past that 70% of emotional sandbagging. It is a self-fulfilling prophecy.

In the 70% there are thoughts like, 'I just know they are going to let me down. I know it is going to go wrong. I know they are going to hurt me,' and even if they didn't you have a self-fulfilling prophecy and you will press their buttons until they let you down.

You will never let go of that 70% of distrust because you are only actually showing 30% commitment to loving yourself and not knowing that Love itself can never be hurt.

The truth is that the graveyards are full of 70% ers. When you are 60, 70, 80 years old you will be saying, 'Why has nobody ever loved me? How come I never truly found love?' and it will be because you believed the wall that you built was true. The wall does not exist though because it is only in your head. If you want to find the Love you want you have got to stop insulting yourself as a loving human being. You are intelligent and you learn from your mistakes and the only unfinished repeated patterns in relationships are the unfinished business of old relationships.

So when you realise that, from today you can actually say, 'I will love openly and fully again the one I am drawn to. I don't wait for any superhuman proof to feel safe before I open up.' Then you will open your heart fully knowing that if they let you down then you will just move on. You know what you want and what you don't want and you move on in trusting love again.

What I am trying to say is you are an intelligent human being and if your heart opens to someone you don't have to immediately sandbag it with all your fears. By doing that you are saying to yourself, 'I don't trust.' It is only your brain that tells you that you are stupid and you are going to make a mistake again.

Your heart never makes mistakes. Only conditional love makes mistakes. Wouldn't life be boring though without all this stuff?!

I know this because this woman has been coming to me for over twenty years, relationship after relationship and as she gets older the makeup gets thicker and thicker and there is a whole visual dance of different hair styles. She is saying to me, 'Will anybody ever love me?'

And I just said, 'No. Not if you believe in that 70% sandbagging. The failure of your relationships is more like a habit than a problem. It is the habituated pattern of believing that your Mind will find love.' Your Mind can never find love. Only Love finds Love.

Your Mind, in its controlling of you, tells you that you know nothing about Love and to distrust it. Your Mind tells you that only it can find the truth. Can't you see that you actually dumb yourself down thinking you don't know what Love is and to distrust it as that thing 'over there'? Truly you are a magnificent intelligent human being and, as I have said, you are not shackled by the experiences of break down and let down in Love.

You know that direction is not real. What I am trying to say is this. What actually happens is that you believe you are dumb and you don't trust the absolute Love within you that has never been hurt, that can never be hurt and never will be hurt.

Instead you pull it down to some low level of corrupted need and want that will imprison you in the needing of love. You are bigger and more magnificent than the 70% sandbagging and you know that in your heart. It is just that you don't want to believe it because you have got friends and people around you living in their 70% shut down saying,

'Love is terrible and hard and difficult and you have to work at it.'

Then they say to you, 'If you have it then it will go.'

They are lying to you, as they lie to themselves, in the suffering which causes empty love. The wall is a darkness which draws you in to conceptualise love itself which in itself is a lie. The only love you ever experience is the mirrored not knowing what Love truly is in Mind's belief.

We don't know what love is because we don't know who we are. The greatest qualification to pursue in life is understanding what Love is in the absolute and very few of us know this because it can only be found through honesty which is a lonely place to be.

## LOVE – THE ANSWER FROM SPIRIT

My Love joins with your Love in Oneness and my Oneness in relationship with itself, an energetic compatibility of natural being of two Spirits, a Love and joy rarely known in this world.

When you Love absolutely you are your Oneness which is Love wrapped in the Oneness of someone else in relationship with itself. That is eternal Love which no man's Mind can ever go to.

When Oneness touches Oneness in absolute honesty and Freedom then we Love and the Oneness is Love touching Love. It is not owned, it is not given but it is forever because it comes from the Forever. It is awakened Love. That is who you are.

And when you say, 'I love you,' in your True Self the heart of God is shared in those words when said from Spirit.

God – it's Monday morning! I hate Mondays! I have got to do the life stuff now.

Where did that Love just go?

Do you get it?

## CHAPTER 9

# THEATRE OF THE MIND

The stories in this book are like a roller coaster taking you down into the darkness of suffering and pulling you up into the light of your Spirit. This is precisely what I want the book to feel like to you because we are all on the roller coaster of Mind's dream.

You know how in every small town you have your local tramp who hangs around outside the supermarkets with a can of beer in his hands or just sits there on a bench and sometimes people sit with him to listen to him and hear the woes of the world and be a 'goody two shoes' to him.

Anyway, there is a town I visit not far from where I live and I had a strange experience with a tramp.

There was a time when I was doing lots of readings in this town and I would keep bumping into this tramp, passing each other like ships in the night, giving each other the look as we passed by each other and engaging for some seconds with a sort of twisted curiosity on both sides. Every time I saw him I just knew I would engage in some kind of conversation with him one day. He always seemed to appear wherever I went and I knew we would talk at some point. He had dishevelled hair, a scruffy beard, raggedy clothes and piercing eyes which scanned everyone that walked past or by him.

One night I was coming out of a house having done an evening of readings and clairvoyance. As I stepped out of the door, standing under the street lamplight like a toothless, capeless Jack the Ripper, was the tramp looking at me. In some calling of destiny the moment had come for us to engage.

He said to me, 'You are that psychic guy, the seer.'

So I answered, 'Kind of.'

I know what's coming next as he says, 'I want to tell you my story.'

So he began the story telling me how when he was 27 years old he had a wife and three children. He was a business man with a nice home and life was going good. He was feeling good. Then suddenly misfortune hit him and he began to drink too much, his wife left him, his business collapsed and he became an alcoholic. Then that became his journey, how he lost everything in that moment in time and at that point in his life. He said, 'All I want to do is be happy and free.'

So there he is standing with his can of beer and I thought, 'He can't get happier than this. He has his can of beer and he is free.' Anyway he continued relentlessly to tell me his story. How he was forced to steal and ended up in prison, every one of his misfortunes, on and on and then he started asking, 'Why?'

I was just listening and looking and then he asked me the question. He said, 'I hear that you help people to find their way. What do you reckon then to my problems, my story?'

So I answered, 'You are asking the wrong person. I don't buy into your hard done to story.'

He started swearing, 'I have had it f**king tough!' He asked again, 'Just tell me what you think.'

So I said, 'Ok. You won't like what you are going to hear but I will tell you what I think.' I said to him, 'You are a Jedi knight.'

He said, 'What's one of them?'

So I answered, 'You are Sir Laurence Olivier. Your belief in your story is so magnificent and your drama is so perfectly rehearsed and acted to perfection that you are a better man than me. I can never be as good as you. You are better than the richest man in this town or the cleverest man in this town. You are the best of the best. I admire you.'

And as I was looking in his eyes I could see his Spirit, this light within him, looking out of this man in raggedy clothes, like a cheeky child looking at me. And my Spirit could see his and feel his and he could see the cheeky child in me.

Then he said, 'But my life has been terrible,' and the light in his eyes changed, his eyes turned back into the eyes of the man he was acting to be. He was the sad sorrowful tramp again.

I said to him, 'You know what I say is the truth. Your act, your performance is so perfect and believed and so deeply profoundly enjoyed in your bizzarest suffering that the Spirit in you jumps in such ecstasy at the perfection of your act. You can feel your Spirit in you and it is alive and smiling and you know everything is alright deep down.'

I said to him, 'You know this don't you?'

Then I looked him in the eyes and said, 'You know Spirit to Spirit that there is nothing wrong with you. I love your acting and so do you.'

And his shining eyes with the cheeky smile said, 'Yes.'

Then I walked off and so did he in the other direction. As he walked away I could see his audience of demons following him like groupies reminding how tough his life is and pulling the shadowed cloak of suffering around him as he walked and began to forget our Spirit to Spirit encounter.

## ARCHETYPES

The other day I was looking on the computer and there is a personality analysis that you can do which then tells you what sort of person you are. Your personality is based on how you answer certain questions and at the end of the questions they then tell you what sort of personality you have. This is then going to be your blueprint for the rest of your life.

It is a bit like astrology with twelve signs and twelve different types of people all with some form of character trait, or should I say archetypes, emotionally and archetypically shaped into a categorised persona. The funny thing is that it seems to work, a bit like Astrology. For myself, I am a Sagittarian and I even look at my own horoscopes occasionally and they seem to fit how I feel, what I do and how I react as if in some magical way they know some truths about me. How strange!

Then it got me thinking, 'What are all these archetypes based upon and founded on? They are usually connected to planets, energy movements or some deep sacred blueprint planted here before we took our first breath.

What I am really trying to say is this. The weird thing is what came first? Was it the archetype from the beginning of your first breathe or did the archetype evolve over time in the evolution of man?

What it really says here is that it takes all these different types of individualised personality that create the emotional, physical and intellectual structure of our society.

Each archetypal personality creates an effect from an emotionally created persona and each different personality causes some form of energetic individuality that resonates in the evolution of this strange, almost eclectic appearing, forming of some twisted purpose called humanity.

Well guess what? All archetypal characters only exist because they have been created by the Mind in its deformed and fractured understanding of itself squaring emotional feelings into identity which we all live and die for. Well I am telling you to step out of the box! You are more wondrous and brilliant than you can ever think.

The thing that you truly are is not an archetypal person and it can never be an archetypal person because only the Mind creates the archetypal Soul personalities. Or perhaps I should say the lab rat effect? Are you the pink rat, the red rat or the orange rat or any other colour you choose?

But isn't it strange how this form of labelling of you as a human being becomes your Soul personality or identity,

'This is your star sign.'

'This is your character.'

'This is your blueprint.'

It all comes back to the same thing which is that you were preordained to be something and to be identified in archetypal personalities as the expression of the Divine.

In general there are twelve different types, although I personally have found sixteen, but you know that you are none of them actually. Only when you know that can you truly manifest from the source of who you are and not the archetypal personality you think you are. The archetypal power is what divides mankind from knowing the true mankind that we are. The archetypal people are the characters in your play, your drama, which only gets reinforced and becomes truth or fact when stamped and approved by death.

## THE TAROT

Many years ago when I was on a mad perfectionist quest of understanding the Tarot I wanted to know what the cards really meant.

What I found within the cards was this confusing gnostic mysticism thrown into the cards by the occultists. The cards were defined in complex multileveled belief systems and each card would have numerology, astrology, kabbalah, auras, runes, colourology, symbology and any other bloody 'ology you can think of.

Each subject was a brilliant stand-alone divinatory system in its own right so you would have to master them all and this in itself would be a life time of studying. It just became so utterly confusing that the cards would never make sense. What I mean by this is that when treating Tarot cards as an eclectic form of divination they became diluted and weak and didn't give respect to stand alone divinatory systems which are deeply powerful.

So I decided to take all that stuff out of the cards and see what was really left. What I found was the story of the archetypal manifestation of human character with all its emotional nuances which would apply to any organised society. What I fully understood after doing thousands of readings was that I could see for whoever was sitting in front of me which archetypal type of personality they oozed identified in their Mind's belief.

I found this to be mind blowingly amazing because then I realised that the Mind itself created the personality from the solid laws of nature but the reality was that a human being defined by the Mind could not hold onto and could not see the whole picture.

So we formed lesser Gods of personalities and from personalities, or archetypal personalities I should say, we then created the numerology, the astrology, the I Ching and any other diagnostic conceptualised habituated patterns of human nature.

But can't you see that all of this evolved through the greater YOU. When I say YOU I mean your Spirit in Mind's dream. Here we sit as a human race divided into all these archetypal character traits which identify us as a human race. We even get people telling us this is your personality and that is what you are going to be until the day you die because it fits your habituated behaviour patterns which were given to you, and told to you, from the moment you were born.by some divine integration of cycled patterns of universal power.

So again life becomes a controlled exercise based upon your preordained archetypal character because that is the best you can ever be. You become judged and labelled by your archetypal personality. But the truth is these categorised and labelled personalities, when lived to their extremes, only ever truly show the passing of your Spirit through the archetypes emotional personality that caused the dance of life ultimately, in another bizarre way, pointing to who you are. For we are all every zodiac sign, we are all every archetypal personality and we will pass through them all in life's longing and then realise that the individualised persona is not who we truly are. That is why you can't take life seriously.

All archetypes are ultimately one and the same voice only becoming individualised strings upon the harp of God's voice. When mankind finally evolves into who we are as Spiritual beings it will be the death of all archetypes. You are not an archetype you are only acting one out. We are more. We are Holy Spirit.

In Shakespeare's words,

*'All the world's a stage*

*And all the men and women merely players.'*

We are all just the actors in this play.

Let's really think about this one.

When I told you the story of the tramp why did I say those words to him and what do you think I really meant? We can only see who we really are when we are still, in awareness and watch this fascinating Vanity Fair.

James Allen said,

*'Mind is the master power that moulds and makes, and man is Mind, and ever more he takes the Tool of Thought, and shaping what he wills, brings forth a thousand joys, a thousand ills. He thinks in secret and it comes to pass; Environment is but his looking glass.'*

These two quotes are very powerful.

Isn't it strange how if we observe ourselves when we are thinking emotionally we create a theatre, a story filled with drama, a play of all that we do which becomes our identity of who we think we are? But the key element is the emotion. Our whole life is driven by emotion wrapped in the survival of the species. We are pure feelings converted by the Mind into an emotional story that becomes the drama of living, acted out in the theatre of nature's elemental creation.

**Earth is our stage where we perform our greatest works in the pursuit of the realisation that we are consciousness in emotional disguise.**

REAL LIFE SOAP

Think of it this way. Imagine tonight on TV there was a soap and the soap was the story of your real life with all the things that are going on in your life, the good, the bad, the dramas, the relationships, the hurts and the illnesses. If the daily routine of your story as you know it was on the TV tonight, I guarantee you this, there would be 20 million people glued to it every night watching, waiting for the next scene, including yourself. You would go, 'This is real life!' Everybody would want to know you, how you would get past the next great love scene or drama and what would happen next. Look at all the people that you pull into your drama, your parents, your friends and your co-workers. What a brilliant story you have got! You would win BAFTA awards and any other drama awards there are.

What we forget though is that we can rewrite the outcome of the next scene once we have exhausted the scene that we are in with all its nuances of suffering, joy and pain.

Imagine you are in the scene and your relationships have gone wrong but you have got a good heart and you struggle with your three kids to get by, hoping for love, always being disappointed and let down. But wouldn't it be funny when you, let's call you Mary, are sitting there thinking, 'My life. Is this is all there is? Is this it? Is this what my life has come to?' and then in the next scene you could write a little miracle which would go something like this;

Mary was walking down the street feeling forlorn and alone but on this particular day she decided to cross the road and go and sit in the square on the bench. Whilst sitting on the bench a random stranger just sat next to her. She looked at him and saw he had gentle eyes and a gentle smile.

He said, 'Are you Mary? I was told by a friend you are really good at making homemade cakes. I am John, by the way, and I have a stall on the market and I am looking for someone who makes homemade cakes. I would like to know your recipes so I can sell them. I will pay you for them.'

From that fortuitous moment it turns out that this man does not have a market stall, in fact he has 100 shops that specialise in unique cakes. He loved cakes just like Mary did. As the journey unfolded so did her career. And she found the man she really loved which was an impossible thing that could never happen in her story of yesterday.

In every one of our plays there is always one little twist we can add that sets us free and becomes our new dream. Life is not just our stage. We are the managers and the creators of the theatre itself, the Spiritual observer that absolutely loves and identifies itself in emotion with the theatre of the Mind creating the most magnificent heart felt plays so brilliant that we become one with consciousness.

So how damn good are you at your play? Doesn't that make you kind of wobble inside because you know there is some truth in that?

## WHO DO YOU LISTEN TO?

When we know who is talking in our heads we can make honest congruent choices in integrity of Spirit.

The problem is which one is talking, your Mind or your Spirit? Yes, your Spirit talks without words but your Mind talks with a million reasons why or why not. The Mind is so noisy in its relentless chatter grabbing your Spiritual feelings and turning them into emotional stories with a past which then becomes your truth, your identity, your persona being continually reinforced by your Mind.

Once it has created addicted codependent proof through emotions experienced in Spirit it becomes the story of who you are forever enforcing itself through its own intellectual, emotional, physical identity of creating and reinforcing our so called Soul personality. This is the thing that you think you are, the Mind that chatters to you every day, wrapped in the endless emotional stories reinforced absolutely by its own judgement which keeps you pissing in the wind till your dead! What I mean is it keeps bringing you back on yourself depending how strong the dream wind is.

I say the dream wind because it is the romantic stories of conspiracy theories, religions, established governments and they are all emotional dummies, or should I say for Americans soothers, drinking off the milk of ego. Have you noticed, or can you even remember, that when you were breast fed as a baby or by bottle you fell asleep. Well it is the same thing. It feeds you until you fall asleep and the sleep feels good until one day you fall asleep and never wake up.

Your Spirit is never, ever asleep. The nearest you get to your Spirit sleeping is lucid dreaming. Lucid dreaming is awareness of your world in non-attachment.

## THE STORYTELLER

The storyteller of your birth, your journey and your death is called your Mind. You are not your Mind but God's magnificence in human form but your Mind does not know that. It looks for it everywhere outside of itself but how can it find what is already here?

It is like being a chair and looking to see if you were a chair. Where do you begin? And how do you know you are a chair? There are many different types of chairs.

This is your Mind talking. This is he who is talking not you. You don't need to talk for the whole world is your voice but you can choose to talk through your physical form.

You are nothing experiencing everything. When Oneness is understood it is nothing. Nothing is Oneness. When you stop travelling in your Mind in thoughts that instantly take you into the future or the past or present, thoughts being formed from feelings being turned into emotion in Mind's story, then you become aware, or should I say awake, which you are right now. You cannot be awake in the future or the past only now in silent witness. When you stop sending your Mind on this journey to understand and find and desire, when you just stop, then you can feel who you are right now.

That is the silent witness within. You are alive and thinking with the Universal Consciousness, or Universal Awareness I should say, without effort or looking or needing or wanting. You are here. You are the eternal Truth. You feel safe just for a while, for a moment, and then your Mind kicks in with its story wrapped in emotion and off you go anywhere but here.

You don't have to be Spiritual to know any of this or have any belief or clever understanding. You are just bloody here! Always! Don't you get it? It is as simple as that. That is IT. Just hold IT for a second and then your true journey begins as a human living not being.

Your Mind is always looking for a story that will create emotion and feelings so the Mind can build its own identity through the emotions and feelings it finds. It relentlessly fights to create Soul personality for if it didn't how would you know that you are alive or be different? It has to make you feel separate in Mind's judgement that holds it all together until one day you get bored to death or experience death from being so bored. As you read this you can feel the something in you. You can feel that this all makes sense. Without 'analysis paralysis' it just feels right.

Your Spirit is actually saying, 'Thank God you can see you are not your Mind. I am who you are. I am your light and life. I am the experience of all experience. I am Freedom breaking free of entrapment. I am always Love that gives rise to being human.'

## FUTILE RESISTANCE

One of my many analogies of how the Mind works is that it is like a main frame computer which is actually a cult with an absolute intention to transform you into the belief that it is perfect so it assimilates you into mini copies of itself in the name of rightfulness but without regard for anything else for it is an emotionless programme of suffering. Its mission is to take all experience and knowledge and claim it as its own. Your Mind is just part of the collective one Mind controlled by a computer that forever learns and adapts so its prime directive can never be changed.

You will be assimilated and resistance is futile. You will become one with the collective emotional duality Mind, perfect and whole. The machine of assimilation is Judgement and the electrical wires in your brain suck out your feelings and turn them into emotional stories which are then fed back into your brain as your story so you believe that you are the

Mind. If you think about this, all that you think and all that you are and all that you do has been assimilated and you will assimilate anyone else around you to be part of you because you are the collective or should I say one ant in a nest of ants. As you talk you can almost feel your Mind grabbing feelings and ideas and assimilating them into reason and belief or non-belief. It is fascinating to experience as an awakened inquiring Spirit without judgement.

When we all talk it is like the Native American Indians used to say in the old films, 'White man speaks with forked tongue.'

It is the tongue of the Mind and the tongue of the Spirit. Just catch yourself when you talk. How much is learnt and remembered nonsense of judgement and how much is said from honest Spirit?

The next question is, 'Which bit comes first?' Usually the voice of the Mind because Spirit only talks if it is really pushed. Let's look at a conversation. Your Mind's voice is always a shouting witness. Your Mind's voice is the entertainer, the ego and the actor viciously overshadowing the voice of your Spirit.

I will give you an example of a conversation which happened in one of my groups.

I asked the group, 'Have any of you got any questions on last week's lesson?'

No one could think of anything and they were just being quiet when one lady said, in a matter of fact way, 'Do you think the alien spaceships are coming down to pick us up in 2012 and save humanity?'

My mind thought, 'What the hell is she taking?!' (This also says a lot about the people I attract in my groups!) I said, 'Well what is supposed to be happening then? Are the aliens coming for us in 2012?'

She said, 'Yes so I have heard.'

Then I asked, 'Who told you that?'

She replied, 'A good friend of mine who channels Ascended Masters.'

My mind is thinking now, 'Ah bless! This is one messed up human being! She has been assimilated by Mind's false comforting dreams from every orifice! In her romantic mind of victimhood some lovely alien is coming to save us. Ah bless! Is she expecting me to have a conversation to affirm this with some other romantic bullshit conspiracy story? So we can dance hand in hand down the garden path of agreed smiled intellectual wonderment of insane unfounded unproven day dreams.'

The fake Mind was talking gibberish out of her mouth wrapped in the voice of her Mind's longing to be loved and feel safe and silenced by fear. Does this make sense to you what I am trying to say? Everyone speaks with a forked tongue hiding their hidden secrets.

Don't get me wrong, if you want to live in your head and believe it to be true then that is fine. What I am saying here is that your Mind is like an arm or a leg, it is just another part of your body and it uses the brain matter to store memory and react to that memory. Your Spirit is none of those things although at the same time it is the power source and the holding form of your Body and Mind. How much garbage do you talk and how much garbage would you live and die for?

## THE MASONS

I was in the Masons for many years and one evening at the festive board, or should I say the meal, a high ranking colleague said to me, 'I hear that you are a clairvoyant for a living.'

This man was always unhappy, angry, judgemental, overeating, over drinking and he was telling me that Spiritual mumbo jumbo is bollocks and how he doesn't believe in any God, which is funny because the main criteria for being a mason is to believe there is a God.

So I said to him, 'The only difference between you and me is that I am happy because my bollocks is more fun than your bollocks!'

When we don't take the Mind seriously it is quite entertaining but when you take the Mind seriously you are being assimilated and run by the collective Mind. What I mean by the collective is the uninformed herd of ignorance.

## INTERPRETING FEELINGS

How good you are at interpreting your feelings makes the importance of your reality.

Your Mind is trying to find the perfect understanding of how you live your feelings in its conceptual control. But whose feelings are they? Are they of your Mind or your Heart? Or maybe both. Are they not both how you identify yourself with who you think you are in your emotional story created from feeling which becomes your habituated codependent fear based identity?

You only identify yourself in your emotional story which your Mind creates. That is its job.

The truth is you are not your emotional story. It doesn't matter how much you want to hold onto it or endorse it or hold it as your life story it is just an emotional story whether it is joyous or suffering.

The moment you stop creating your story built on emotional experience and memorised experiences then you become free because the truth of who you are is the feeling of Spirit.

The Spirit feels its existence through living form but it feels without a story. It doesn't hold onto its feelings, it is just forever experiencing them, love or suffering, it just experiences them without a story. This is the glory of flowing in one with all things. It is only when your Mind grabs the feelings and adds a story to them that it becomes an emotion, a memory of a past and a potential future identified in time. The emotional story is forever reinforced creating your persona or who you think you are in addictive behaviour.

The energy of the Mind, when taking feelings then holding them and turning them into emotional experiences, whether good or bad, is the hotwiring of memory.

Then what of learning? You didn't learn to breathe, your heart didn't learn to beat and you didn't learn how to think you were only told what to think. Only your Mind learns to understand and the power of the understanding of the Mind is how it is triggered emotionally which then becomes hotwired as memory.

We are all barking mad telling everyone we are normal in our conformity to our Mind's story.

If you only just sensed for one second that there is a whole real you, a Spiritual being which has no bonds or boundaries that is intelligent and aware which knows your whole life, then you would know the person that you are and have always been.

When I say person I don't mean a personified person, I mean this vibrant shining Spirit of love that you are without question.

You can never be a person. You are Oneness, only felt and seen and known in silent awareness which is at your core always calling you to know the selflessness that you are but we have forgotten this because Mind has claimed us. It is hard to let go of our identity and our story wrapped in the emotions of proof because we fear there is nothing else. And the Mind says, 'That's right. There is nothing else.'

I tell you there is this thing within you, your Spirit, whose story is more beautiful, more absolute and forever and it is full of Love.

That is what you feel and see and know when you find the courage and the faith to let go of your story. You do not even have to find it. It will present itself to you the moment you honestly truly let go. And you can do that this very second if you have the courage to do so.

## COURAGE

There are two types of courage. There is courage of your Mind and courage of your Spirit.

Courage of the Mind is a programmed ability to face danger or pain when upon the battlefield of life. Mind's courage starts very strong but falters and weakens and then you become prey of the enemy of Spirit which is Judgement. Then you become submissive to the beast of the Mind and its many mansions and your courage turns into the feelings of empty purpose so allowing the cruel world to continue being the God of greed, tradition and religion.

Mind's courage always feels empty, like acting out your part in the play then waiting for your applause in a twisted need for approval.

Courage of the Spirit is never called for. It bursts out of us when injustice threatens the humanity that we are. It is the power of Love, so intense and bright it will pick you up from the dirt and fill you full of strength and purpose to face danger, fear and pain knowing that this eternal silent power, absolute kindness of love and joy, holds this burning sword of fire that will chop down and dismantle all injustice of the Mind without reason only in the name of Love. It is a force that will pick you up, that enlightens you and shows the world the Angel that you are.

Against all odds it is the power of not wanting, the power of your Holy Spirit being freed and making an example to the jackal of Judgement.

Courage is the consistent silent witness of the honest heart standing for what is right from the centre of Heart's Love. It knows what it gives comes from the Holy Spirit in righteousness. True courage can't be found or created. It jumps out of you in the face of any injustice against Spirit. Its resonance stays in your Heart until it brings freedom from oppression. You can trust and feel this silent courage within that always beckons you to live your life in the open heart of everlasting love and strength. Courage is found in you every day by feeling its simple joyous awareness of its power calling you like some beautiful distant voice, far way away in your Mind but making your heart and stomach feel warm with unknown courage. The awakened love that you are defends Love and any Love that resides in all humans and all things without question.

When we speak with the conviction of Spirit, not the assertiveness of reason, that true courage is the God within you saying, 'That is enough.

## THE FOREVER

The Forever is who I am. It is always here within me and everything I see is the Forever too. It is everything I say and do. It is every thought and every feeling being held in the Forever. You and I are the Forever. It is Love, freedom and joy held in the Forever's hands whose hands are the Forever too. Even writing this is the Forever. It is aliveness smiling in the Forever.

Your Spirit is Forever's Love manifest. Its touch is joy feeling itself. Your voice is its Song of Eternity. Your blood and bones are its temporary dwelling place made by the Forever. Your Mind paints the Forever in Mind's dream, your eyes see its colours and your feelings remember its passing held in Mind's drama and passions. What dies is the story created by the Forever as it moved through form.

Your first breath is the Forever awakened in awareness of itself being the ultimate expression of the magnificence of living life. Being awake is the silent Forever alive in you. When we recognize the Forever then Mind's duality becomes rich with honest purpose not suffering created by Mind's judgement.

The Forever is all that has been, all that is here now and all that will be. We are the Forever.

# CHAPTER 10

# KARMA & PAST LIVES

If you have never experienced a guided meditation then go and do one! Guided meditations are amazing!

I can remember the first time I ever did a guided meditation it was wonderful. There I was going on this journey into a sacred place with beautiful waterfalls and scenery and high frequency energy, where I could go to a place by a waterfall and be washed clean of all my sadness and sorrows. For this was a healing waterfall in a paradise garden

Then I would walk from the waterfall to the sacred grove where I would meet my Spirit guide, some Angel or Spirit guide of great love and wisdom.

They would talk to me and tell me how precious I was. How much they loved me and how they were there for me. This was a great place to be, balancing and healing all my chakras, at peace with my Spirit in this wondrous brilliant Angelic world. This was a good place to be. A place of great promise and when I was brought back in my body into my awake world on a grey miserable rainy day how could I not, as a human being after having had such an experience, feel that there was something far grander than me in the world. I began to realise I was a divine Spirit of God. This was good stuff! Stuff you want to share with the world.

After about a year or two of regular meditation and this escape into my Mind's dream and high frequency reaching up to Spirit, I went through many different types of guided meditations and even past life meditations. I danced around the fires with Native American Indians, went to Heaven and held hands with Angels, swam in the blue oceans of Atlantis, sat on top of Tibetan mountains with High Priests, felt my blueprint of purpose and sat upon the surface of Mars. I had been in the tombs of the dead in the pyramids, been a shape shifter in the forests and sat with my ancestors. The list goes on.

I would open my eyes feeling good and empowered. but here I was every day, through my work, hearing the suffering and needs and wants of humanity. And I myself was struggling to survive and hold a family together. This was a new kind of conditioning leading me down many roads of Spirituality but if I was honest there was still something missing. Something not quite right which no words could describe. There was just something missing. Maybe one day in a meditation one of my guides would give me the answer to what was missing and how to save the world. I was still living in the world like everyone else trapped in survival of need and want but I had a new cloak to wear, a cloak of Spiritual understanding.

## KARMIC DEBT

I had become one of those Spiritual types, or to the normal people, Spiritual fruit loops! But inside there was this silent witness which I could not touch and did not really understand. There was just something.

Did this in fact make my life better or more full of purpose? No. In fact these were the times that led to great suffering and struggle in my life. These were times of divorce and breakdown and my life being turned upside down. Then I was being told by people, spiritual people, 'This is God punishing you,' or 'He is teaching you a lesson.'

So being me, and always rethinking and reseeking the truth in this stuff, I came to the conclusion that there is no God in heaven and we are not paying for past life karma only living in historic karma. We have not come here to learn lessons and to be punished and we have not chosen our parents. It was all a pile of croc if I was honest. They were all great plasters over the weeping wounds of life's perilous journey. These were all just great justifications of an unsaid truth.

I realised it was an insult to humanity and the Spirit within us and I realised we are all God in disguise, this magnificence in human form, but how could I prove or show this?

Then I remembered sitting in one of many Spiritual groups with diverse types of people from hippies to scientists all on a Spiritual path. This Spiritual group with all their various beliefs in Angels, power, energies, all talking about the causes of man's suffering and man's inhumanity to man just felt like blah blah blah to me. We were all spiritually talented in our fields, Reiki masters, crystal healers, energetic healers, chakra experts, holistic medicine - a whole pile of 'goody two shoes'. So today I thought, 'I will rock the boat and break that cycle of pretended concern.'

I said, 'There is no God in Heaven.'

Then I said to them, 'I will tell you the reason why I said that. Do you honestly believe if you sat in Heaven with JC, Allah, Mohamed, Buddha or any other Ascended Gods and got your notepad out and said, "This is going to be my story, my blueprint. I am going to have crap parents, crappy job, shit relationships and be victimised. What do you reckon God? Do you think that will do for me?"

Can you imagine saying that to God?! Let's be honest what would you write? To be honest you would probably be too busy looking good! All the money, all the goods, all the chicks in the world, anything you wanted and die a hero loved by the world. Anyway, so my story was the bad one. Bit like yours eh?

So, on the way down from Heaven having written my preordained story of suffering I had no say because I had already done it. The programme was worked out and as I was falling from Heaven towards the Earth God said, "By the way son, when you are down there I am going to punish you some more just in case."

I said, "Ok God that's fine."

And God said, "I haven't finished yet. I am going to make you learn lessons while you are down there, hard lessons and hard knocks of life," and as I was falling God said, 'and I will give you some karma. You can pay for some past life karma crap. You will get punished all the way."

So I said "God that sounds pretty grim."

Then God said, "One last thing. Your parents are going to be arseholes and you are going to be born into whatever is the most persecuted race at the moment."

No wonder the first thing you do is scream when you are born! You have just been dropped in to the combat zone of life!' (The beginning of identifying ourselves through fear and suffering.)

On reflection, if I am God and magnificence in human form, Spirit consciousness of Oneness then this is the biggest insult to your Spirit and humanity.

You are free and your Spirit has not come to learn any lessons for you already know everything. You didn't write a story because there are no roads to the truth that you are. We are not preordained lab rats. We are more beautiful and wondrous than you can ever imagine. We are pinnacles of creation. Free Spirits dancing the Forever in the Forever's boundless love.

You didn't come here to be punished. How can you be if you are eternal? How can you pay for past life karma you can't even remember? You can only be born into historic karma. You are already the accumulation of life's longing to be. You didn't choose your parents either. You could have been born to a family starving to death in Africa or to the

President of America. You could have been born whole or deformed but you were going to be born.

Living Consciousness will hold itself in any living organic form as long as it can hold that life force. For are you not the very breath of Gods breathing Spirit? You are free will. You are the mystery taking a breath.

So let us not insult ourselves as some monkey evolved species with a brain shoved in the top so we can walk around until we croak all for nothing. You are the most beautiful thing that God could ever come up with. YOU. Doesn't that make conspiracy theory sound stupid?

So let us all break out of this conceptualised identity in Spirit imprisonment. We are all the omnipresent brilliance of the God within us.

Some people may be thinking. We are all brothers and sisters and the people who came to hurt us most of all in this life chose to and it was agreed upon in heaven with JC when they were doing their blueprint stuff and genetic code and all that crap! And do you know why they came to punish you? It is because they love you! The next time round you reverse roles. I suppose you can work out how good you can whip their arse when they get down here when it's their turn. That story only does one thing for you. Even though it is not true it helps you to forgive and let the guilty go free which is a good thing.

Karma is the forgotten lies of yesterday that are paid for in suffering by the ignorant. It is the unfinished business of world sadness which in itself is a lie which can never be sorted because it lives in the justification of the lie itself that only feeds emotional judgement creating the emotional theatre of the Mind in the heart of suffering, forever to be paid back.

# CHAPTER 11

# THE GOD OF JUDGEMENT

We all have disappointments, let downs and blames. Blaming others, blaming ourselves and blaming the world that has caused us suffering all judged on the moral ground. When disappointment is not understood it turns into resentment. When resentment is not released then it turns into grievance which will not let go of you because its best friend Judgement holds its hand.

This is what labels and kills the love in yourself and the person or people who truly love you. The Grudge Judge is the enemy of our Spirit and the greatest friend of ego. How often we feel hurt or disappointed when what we expect doesn't happen and what we expect is one of the greatest things called expectation.

Expectation is the soil where grievance's seed grows wrapped in its shell of judgement. When it grows and flowers each petal is a labelling and it is full of thorns and dark but it lives. Isn't it strange how a grudge turns into a grievance and the grievance is a solidification of judgements, a personal form of conceit, but in awareness they are all energies, all supporting and creating energy that is so strong it makes us react in the physical form to do things that cause suffering to others and ultimately to ourselves.

What people don't know is that Judgement is an energy which is real and so is the emotional ground of expectation it grows in.

There are two kinds of Judgement. There is honest judgement which is like when you are crossing the road and if there is a car coming the other way if you don't get out of the way you will get knocked over.

Then there are all the emotional judgements of the Mind which are the power house for twisting our perception of reality. And also one of Judgement's other best friends is called our past or history and as we all know history is usually written by the victors in their arrogance created by grievance and the personal form of conceit which is Judgement. The past can only justify its own truths.

Wow where did that come from?! Got all serious there for a minute! I guess some God stuff is trying to push through but you know it makes sense. Just another quick thought that's all it was for a moment.

I only say this because it has resonated in my own life, where I have been judged for my inaccuracies and my inability to understand other people's feelings. That is another thing. When expectation holds your hand it always leads to your disappointment because expectation is just all your fears being controlled by Judgement itself. You can never give a rational answer to the Grudge Judge. While sitting in the interrogation room of the Grudge Judge you can only give a reactive answer, which in itself is only confused nonsense to give yourself more time to think how to deal with this labelling, which then makes you a liar.

EMOTIONAL JUDGEMENT

Once we are born we are taught by our loved ones, our community and our cultures to judge on some factual moral ground which slowly cloaks us in forgetting the Love that we are. The one thing that stops us from being One and truly alive is the energy of Judgement. Judgement needs to be observed. Observe how the energy of Judgement feeds off you. It is the Mind's greatest tool of deception. It is the fear that arises within you and robs you of being one with your true Spirit.

Judgement is the master builder of fear based suffering and identity. Judgement is another demon of the physical form and it stops you being fully present. It is the imprisonment and bars of your loving Spirit. We die in all the given and taken judgements of ourselves and others which is the suffering and pain of life's duality.

Death is the end and final judgement. Death is only the one time Judgement feels its own pain and suffering in our return back to full Oneness. When I say death is judgement's only felt suffering that is because at the time of death Judgement suffers because it has no more power and it is the end of its control and story.

Judgement in physical expression and emotional form becomes narcissism in sociopathic behaviour.

Judgement is arguing the argument that no one really believes. It is the theatre of the Mind and Judgement takes feelings then turns them into an emotional lie creating your story of who you think you are. Judgement wears the cloak of suffering.

The bizarre thing is when the emotional Mind judgement, not reality judgement, is held and its story (which is many layered) is removed, at the very bottom it reveals the hidden calling of Love. Judgement is the hidden secret of Love. When you strip Judgement away what is actually left is sacred Love. Letting go of Judgement stops the imprisonment of others and of the love within you.

It also is your false Higher Self and the silent words wrapped in survival's fear. The moment we fear for our survival then Judgement kicks in. Why? To find what you desire at any proven cost.

Judgement tarnishes all beauty and invalidates all dreams. It takes whatever thought you feel good about that is beautiful and amazing, that has no beginning and no end, that is just beautiful and then the Mind's judgement wraps around it and leaves it empty and you can't even remember what you dreamed.

Judgement corrupts and builds the wall and darkness that stops you from seeing the light that you are and it is so convincing in belief which is one of Judgement's most precious shields. The light that you are only becomes a concept never to be felt or believed.

Judgement and blame are friends. Both are self - justifications of the truth and they are personal forms of conceit. It is the fear we build our world on making all of us live fear based lives.

## THE DEMON OF JUDGEMENT

If Judgement had a body:

Its Mind would be the jury of twelve which is Vanity, Cynicism, Humiliation, Pride, Narcissism, Desires, Time, Envy, Hope, Guilt, Expectation and Greed.

Its Eyes would be the cold eyes of Criticism.

Its Ears would be deaf and never hear the cries for mercy.

Its Nose would only smell death, fear and sorrow.

The Mouth would talk lies and illusion.

Its Right Hand would be fear

Its Left Hand would be pain.

Its Feet would stand upon twisted morality

And the fire in its Stomach would feed on the death of life's longing.

The blood in its veins would be your fear based purpose that motivates you into living your life as a lie.

When you are possessed by this Demon it sucks your strength and faith, dreams and life force and creates the drama and persona of the warmongers of fear and control, like a toxic goo leaving you shell shocked and not knowing who you are.

It is pretty grim stuff I know and in our bizarre way we wrap 'love and light' around it hoping to heal it and fix it but it is always there waiting. It is that thing that when you think you have got your life fixed and sorted, even when you have found your wisdom, it still sits in its cocoon waiting to come out at some point. Only death can kill it, either death of duality or the death of your physical form.

## THE BIRTH OF SIN

On reflection I have lived a life looking for approval and disapproval from the people who I thought understood me and loved me the most. This was the beginning of the imprisonment of my power and of the child within held in Judgement's arms. And we suckle off its ego breasts like innocent babies which in itself is the milk of approval and disapproval.

It always tastes sweet but like sugar it kills you. Judgement is the voice of duality. Judgement is the biblical Devil. Judgement is the thief's justification.

How do I see this stuff that I am telling you? When I was a child I was a free Spirit, living in a house full of lodgers with no one telling me right and wrong. Not even my mom telling me right or wrong. What I experienced was just how it was and there was no emotional Mind's judgement.

I remember one day in particular when I was playing in the garden with my friends and my mom called me in and said to me, 'Don't talk to the lady on the left hand side of us. She is a nasty piece of work, keep away from her.'

I never asked why so that was the truth to me because my mom was right. She was the grown up and they knew everything.

Then the same day my mom called me back in again and she told me, 'The lady on the right hand side, she is a lovely old lady. Be kind to her. Help her do her shopping and cut her grass. She will even pay you 6d for doing it.'

Again I accepted because my mom was always right. Then I was off again playing with my friends in the garden, lost in the world of cowboys and Indians and soldiers.

Then she called me in again and said, 'I have got someone to talk to you about God.'

He was one of mom's lodgers who was a priest, I think he was catholic, and he started talking to me about sin and Jesus and right and wrong. I was just a kid and he said to me, 'You are a sinner.'

As a seven year old I thought, 'What the hell is he talking about? What is sin? What is that word?'

But because he was a man of the cloth he was the truth, a grown up and even more so because he was from the church. He said, 'The only way you can be saved is by being a servant to Jesus Christ and being a good boy and doing what your parents tell you. Otherwise you will go to hell.'

Well for a seven year old that was pretty big stuff! So anyway, after my lecture of Heaven and Hell and how I was a born sinner, I went out to play in the garden with my four friends and I said to them, 'You're a sinner, you're a sinner, you're a sinner and you're a sinner,' and it was the truth because God told me.

On reflection, the whole event was just another day when I was robbed of my truth and told to distrust the loving Spirit that I am in Judgement's Mind. It's as mad as believing we have boundaries and borderlines that are real which define our countries when in truth there is only one world, one people. When we let go of emotional Judgement peace will fill the Earth.

Judgement is our convincer that our story is true at any cost. Some of the greatest words of Judgement are, 'That is the fact. That is the truth,' but if we know our story isn't true, not ever, then Judgement has no power. Judgement isn't the condemner of the crime; Judgement is what the crime is born from. Judgement is our hidden secret, even though our whole world around us suffers in Judgement.

## THE GRIEVING GRIEVANCE

When a grudge which is an injustice of yesterday's expectations becomes so deeply embedded it becomes a grieving grievance. This is Judgement's food and it is ugly. It is only when we let go of Judgement, when we let the guilty go free, that everyone is freed to be the truth that they are. The guilty are guilty because the bars of Judgement needs prisoners for its jail built from fear and suffering made in the law of separation. If emotional Judgement didn't exist there would be no crime.

Expectation is Judgement in disguise which is beginning to tell us something here, that the whole lot is a package, a story, that isn't who you are.

I know because Judgement has ravaged my life or should I say my life force but it can't destroy it for it is eternal.

Judgement twists Love's beautiful truth. The opposite of Judgement is non-judgement and in non-judgement is love, truth and the light but our Judgement is so deeply embedded in us that we can't really believe those words, they just became a concept again.

Judgement has no holding on peace. So when Jesus says, *'Peace be with you.'* He is saying that in peace there is stillness and silent awareness from Spirit which has no duality or Mind's emotional Judgement. In peace we are free of judgement.

## LEFT THE CHURCH NOT CHRIST

Again when I was a young man, there have been times in my life when I diligently went to church with a big open heart. I loved the words of Jesus but I found it difficult to follow the religion realising religions are built on the twisted words of men not the words of Christ.

For example, we would go to people's houses to proselyte, telling people how the drunk and the addict in the street is full of sin and the only way to be saved from this wicked world is through Jesus Christ.

But it kind of didn't add up. The words of Jesus saying,

*'Love your neighbour as yourself,'*

but then the religion of men saying, 'They are wicked. That's why they are like that. They are full of the Devil'

In my mind I was thinking, 'Aren't we all God's children?'

The moment I actually said, 'I don't think that this is true. They are no different from us. They are beautiful Spirits.'

Then they said, 'How can you say that? We are the chosen ones, the righteous ones.'

So I said, 'Isn't even what you are saying elitism?'

And then they turned on me and said, 'That is the Devil talking in you. You should not question the lord your God.'

What they were really saying was that man's religion is held together by elitist blind faith and must dare not ever be questioned. Any religion or men full of true faith would never resent or fear questioning for their loving hearts are full of the Holy Spirit. There is nothing to fear and nothing to hide.

That is why I have no fear in questioning any religion or prophet or God because I can't accept the blind faith of religious judgement but when we hear the words of Christ himself, like other great prophets who talk of Spirit and through Spirit, then their truth is undeniable. That is why I can love the purity of true prophets whether Buddhist, Muslim, Christian or Jew or any other faith because they all speak with the same tongue, the tongue of Love absolutely.

I was told if anyone questions this religion in any shape or form then that is the Devil talking and I realised that was the lie.

That is why I left the church but not Jesus Christ.

## THE BIRTH OF JUDGEMENT

Going back to the force of Judgement and the energy of Judgement, the day we took the God within us out of ourselves and put him into the sky in Mind's dream then Judgement was born. We have to try to observe how we react to its energy as physical beings.

Judgement services our genetic physical need to survive and be and procreate for the survival of the species. Judgement is there, solid like a rock. It will make sure that you eat the other animal and this judgement will keep you alive. It will say you need fire and warmth and that becomes an emotional judgement too because warmth means feelings.

Then we have all the emotional judgements like, 'I love you, I hate you, I need you and I can't live without you,' and all that kind of stuff.

There are Intellectual judgements like, 'I am clever, you are stupid, I know how things work and you don't.'

The Mind's Judgement always creates a sense of power. Whether intellectual, physical or emotional it creates this fear based power.

When I talk of duality I don't mean Mind and Spirit I mean the Mind itself is duality. Don't forget that. Judgement is your duality. Spirit is totally separate. Duality of the Mind is the penny, heads and tails, and what the Mind creates is your Soul personality. Your Soul personality is built upon Judgement and conditioning which then creates the story and the drama of the whole of your life but it is not who you truly are, it is just a dance. You are also your Spirit. And here is the bizarre twist. Spirit created your Mind, Body and Judgement and all that manifests in our world for without Spirit there would be no life. This is showing there is purpose to existence so Spirit itself can know in the energy of feeling what it is. (Who's talking?)

Who is more crippled? The man with no legs or the man who cannot take another step in his sadness, guilt and suffering? Which one is in the most pain?

The man with no legs can get a wheelchair and people will help carry him. He has an answer or he will pull himself forward by his hands showing great will to live. The man crippled by Mind's judgement is actually already dead or, should I say, just waiting to die.

Who, or what, saves him? What faith or conviction can save him? The answer is, 'Don't take life so bloody seriously!' Judgement is the most serious dude on the block! So serious we go to war and kill each other!

## FIXING ANALYSIS PARALYSIS

The other way is giving in and acceptance. Yes you are the biggest wretched failure that the world ever did see and here is another bizarre twist. So for any of you reading this we are going to fix your 'analysis paralysis' right now in Mind's Judgement.

If you are overweight just say to yourself, 'I am the fattest ugliest person you ever did see!'

If you lie then say to yourself, 'I lie because I am the biggest liar the world has ever seen!'

If you have no money then you say to yourself, 'I am so broke I haven't got a pot to piss in or a window to throw it out of!'

Bring it all out!

'My family hates me because I am the biggest loser you ever did see.'

'I just realised that my wife, who I thought was my only love, has had more men than I have had hot dinners!'

'I have got allergies to everything you can think of.'

'I hate flying in case the plane might crash.'

'I am too old. I feel like a thousand years old!'

I want you to really bring forward in front of you now all the things that you think are wrong with you, and the world, but especially yourself. Then add even more stories to it. Make it worse than it has ever been, 'Tomorrow your house will be broken into, your children will be will be abducted by aliens, your grandparents will be held for ransom by terrorists and there is an imminent earthquake about to hit you followed by a tsunami and the world is on the brink of World War III.'

Just keep adding to your misery. If you want to do misery then let's do it good! If you want to do Judgement then let's go all the way.

Just keep adding to it and then keep adding again. Do it for an hour' do it for month. How bad it is going to get and how bad it has been. If you are going to feed Judgement and suffering then let's give it all the food it wants and all the emotion it wants. Throw yourself on the floor and cry like a baby! Hold the agony in your heart and get more of it. See if you can burst your heart with this agony. Love your victimhood!

Scream at the top of your voice, 'Come and get me then Devil! I'm not scared of you! Come on God kill me then!' and mean it!

Shout out, 'I am the most worthless wretch the world has ever seen. There is nothing I can do that is right! I am sin! I am challenging you God!'

And do you know, isn't it funny, there is a point that you come to where there are no more words or thoughts. They are exhausted and it just all stops. Suddenly it all becomes meaningless and pointless.

It is just an endless raving, emotional shouting to exhaustion and when you fill it up with more of that it just suddenly has no meaning. And there is a silence, a strange empty solidness and you are still here and there is no Judgement and blame. And you know all the things about yourself are not really true. You know it is not you. It is like the end of the story.

Welcome home. There are no more thoughts or words just YOU. You might just feel like laughing from Spirit. And laughing at the absurdity of what you believed to be true so honestly that you physically lived it. It is like a joyous Spirit that is in you but can't be touched. Welcome home. There is no suffering without its story. There is no persona without Judgement. There is no memory without feeling. There is only love and joy and freedom when you let go in acceptance that all that IS, is temporary but all that you ARE is forever.

Where is this home?

This home can never be found externally through desire. Everyone is looking outside of themselves to find the Love, their success, their peace, their fulfilment. We all do that ceaselessly. One day we will get things right and then we will be happy. Guess what? It has never happened yet since the dawn of man. There is no external desire that has ever brought true happiness and freedom but only another form of absolute believed drama believing our story to be true. The only freedom and truth and love that is forever and safe and empowering is already in us but we just don't believe it because we have got to ask the judgement Mind.

We are looking for our Mind to fix our problems and to find the answer to our lives because we really believe our Mind is so clever that it will find the way out. Even though in our heart we are still sad and suffering we believe our Mind will find the answer but in fact it is the cause of our suffering. The truth is it will never find the answer. We are not our Mind and the person that it creates, even though it reinforces every day this thing we call our self. We are a person, a creature created by Judgement.

How do you pull the plug on your Mind? To put it simply you just pull the plug on the robot that runs your life. And how it is done is 'Just stop going there. Just don't go there.' The plug is going there and pushing it into the socket that powers it up.

## WHO IS DRIVING THE CAR?

It is very difficult to live in a world where everyone you talk to is not real. They are mere robots that self-perpetuate their own story and become a free roaming robot totally absorbed in acquiring until it is dead.

To give you another analogy, I was driving behind a car the other day and it made me think, 'Who is driving the car?' This was one of those expensive cars with a personalised number plate being driven by someone who has got 'Success.' It is hard to explain that the whole Mind of that person driving the car is this robot believing itself to be alive and in control, an individualised free roaming robot programmed to acquire. It is scary to realise there was no real human being driving the car but a pure duality Mind following all the rest of the cars with separated duality Minds. How scary is that? We are all anatomical machines roaming the Earth consuming everything with some madness or, should I say, a bizarre programme of survival and desire without batteries. I say this because the majority of people I talk to are not there. They are just talking robots with conviction. How can you ask this programmed robot of acquisition, power and control to understand humility?

When you ask this robot, 'How do you feel? What do you want?' it spews out this brilliant story of ego and even the human that this voice is coming from knows in their heart that it is not them that is talking but this habituated robot voice telling you what you need and who you are on some moral ground it does not know.

A bit like a soap opera it is just a whirlwind of judgement, emotions, anger and resentment all fighting for some moral ground which doesn't know what it is.

Guess what the moral ground is? It is Judgement with expectation.

## MORAL GROUNDS OF JUDGEMENT

The moral grounds are the laws of Judgement. The purpose of this book is for you to observe the process you go through in your Mind to manifest and create your reality and then after that to assert it as a fact.

When the fact is just you talking it then you are belligerent; when a group of you have the same facts then you become a gang; when all the gangs join together they become a nation and when two different nations bump into each other with their facts then the God of judgement goes to war.

Another analogy is if you give a man a gun he has a say. If that man kills ten people then he is a murderer. If he joins up with ten other men who have guns then he has a gang who controls the community. If that gang grows with their beliefs joining other gangs with similar beliefs then they become an army and when you kill a thousand people you become a conqueror.

All of the suffering world is created by the Mind, the Mind of survival at any cost. Your Mind is always slowly claiming you again and assimilating you with its Judgement. Mind is nothing but Judgement and when I say the Mind is nothing but Judgement it is absolute Judgement.

It is not the clever thing that helps you create or be inspired or see the beauty of the world because that does not belong to your Mind. Those things belong to passion of Spirit. The Mind is a cruel entity for survival empowered by emotion which in itself it creates endlessly. The suffering Mind is the Mind of Judgement. Your real Mind is egoless and full of light and creative potential. The other Mind, you can call is your persona Mind, your personality Mind which is who you think you are, is created by

Judgement itself. Is not your personality only Judgement when you break it down?

Isn't all drama just Judgement created in the story of drama? This is only what you choose to dance with not who you truly are.

Let's get this clear. Your Mind is Judgement. The Mind that questions what you believe in its incessant criticalness is the Mind only. It is the bully to your Spirit. It is the bully. This big thing called your Mind is tiny but it feels bigger than anything in the world. It tells you what to do, who you are and the story it gives you is built on its Judgement.

Even your clever thoughts which are grown from Judgement and comparison are your Mind. If you removed your Mind just for a second you would understand that you possess the vastness and intellect of the conscious universe within you always. That is your divine right and who you are.

# CHAPTER 12

# UNFINISHED BUSINESS OF CHILDHOOD SADNESS

All your personal relationships are mirrors of the unfinished business of childhood sadness. All your hidden fears and strengths are also the unfinished business of childhood sadness.

I know some of you reading this might think, 'I had a great childhood, a normal family and a privileged life,' but the same still applies to you because the unfinished business of negative childhood experience and feelings is the resonance of your hidden fears that build your personality. Whether it is good or bad, whether it is rich or poor, it is the fertile ground of you living your half lived life that is built from your hidden secrets.

I don't mean weird secrets or bizarre secrets I mean the hidden secrets of how you want your Love back of who you are, safe in a world which honours and knows that Love, that real Love that we never actually truly talk of, that Love that was robbed from us and cruelly crushed and shadowed in the desires of the world. It is a sadness that we cannot put a finger on, something that has been taken from us, the thing that is missing.

## THE SHADOWS BIRTH

What has gone is the absolute Love that we are but it hasn't really gone it has just been overshadowed by the cloaks of judgement, sadness and fear. Childhood sadness is the sadness of how we are pulled away from the innocent Love that we are into codependent love of the Mind forced upon us by our parents in their false understanding of love leaving a shadow of fear which we cannot make sense of. However that shadow manifests it becomes our emotional yardstick for all our relationships in future life. If you look carefully at your own relationships at the moment they are your fearful emotional Mind's reflections being played out in securing or finding the Love you lost in a dramatised codependent game of life.

Unknowingly what we are looking for is the answer to our lost innocent Love through the people around us. To bring this into a human concept we need to look at what happens when this manifests in the people we trust and love.

I once had such a partner. I trusted her in my sadness and told her so much about myself and opened up in my honesty all my weaknesses and my fears. This person was a so called great 'healer psychologist' and when she felt angry or fearful she used it against me. In the guise of the 'healer' she attacked my beliefs and all that I held dear, making me feel my strengths were in fact my weaknesses, making me feel that I was wrong to create my own life. I also have older brothers and a sister who did the same in childhood and so I questioned myself in believing they were right and I was wrong in some bizarre trust in them.

After thirty years of this I had lost real direction and power within myself to build my life and live congruently. This disappointment caused the feeling within me that I was always wrong and didn't deserve love. Strangely enough this repeated pattern of approval and disapproval was perpetrated on me as a child which I reinforced later in adult life by pulling in codependent relationships unknowingly reflecting the unfinished business of that childhood sadness.

That relationship was a masterpiece of such emotional complexity played out in both of us which reflected the deep loss of the natural Love we had as children which was torn away from us. As children we had no yardstick or understanding of relationships, we just accepted what happened to us in hidden disbelief, like an invisible shadow which would then follow us all of our days.

## BORING HUSBAND

Anyway, I want to share with you one peculiar experience I had. This was a day at a very popular important Spiritualist church which was usually filled with over a hundred people. After doing my service, or towards the end of it, there was a lady in the front row I was particularly drawn to. She was a well-dressed middle aged woman and as usual I was inspired and drawn to flow with my consciousness and awareness in a free flowing communication.

So I said to this lady, 'I have a very strong clairvoyant connection with you but this is about your personal relationship with your husband and I don't think it would be appropriate for me to go into why I have been drawn to this connection with you on a personal level. I suggest that you come to me later on after this service and have a private reading with me because I have a message for you which is of great importance.'

Then the woman said, 'No. I am happy for you to communicate with me now.'

I replied, 'Are you sure you want to in front of all these people because it is going to be very personal?'

With her brazen voice she said, 'I don't have anything to hide.'

So I said, 'OK. We will begin and if you feel uncomfortable then we will stop.' I continued, 'What I see is that you have two men in your life. One is your husband and the other one is someone else you are very drawn to. You can see where I am going with this. Do you really want me to continue with this or would you prefer to see me later?'

'No that is fine,' she said 'I have nothing to hide and no secrets.'

I said to her, 'You are a very brave woman in front of all these people,' and I carried on, 'What I see here psychically, and with Spiritual energy connecting with you, is that you have a husband who is feeling pushed away but I don't feel that he is a bad man. Also there is another man in your life you may have known for a long time and you are feeling pulled to this man who you have connections with.'

Then I continued saying, 'What I feel with your husband is that there is a very real dislike in you even though, as I said, I feel in my heart that he is not a bad person. Also I feel that you have been married for twenty years and you have been together a long time.'

'No I haven't been married twenty years,' she said, 'it is twenty one years.' '

Well,' I said, 'that is close enough for me and his name is Matthew. Is that right?'

She said, 'Yes his name is Matthew.'

Then I added, 'This other man you are linked to is called Andrew.'

She looked surprised, 'How did you know that?' she asked.

I replied, 'Isn't that what you are here for, to talk to a psychic? That is my job.' I continued, 'There is a very big concern of energy around you connecting to your husband. You want him gone, even to the point of almost hating him.'

'Too right,' she said, 'he is the most boring twit under the sun!'

All the women in the congregation made that sound, 'Ah! I can't believe she just said that in front of all these people! She called her husband a boring twit!'

This kind of talk had certainly never been heard before in the church.

I said, 'Really? And what else?'

'He watches eight hours of TV a day,' she said.

'Is that true?' I asked.

And she replied again, 'Too right!'

I said, 'So basically you want to leave him and be with this other man. Are you sure you want to go on with this? It is very personal and everyone is very intrigued to know what happens next.'

The woman said, 'I just can't stand him anymore. He is boring, he watches TV all day long and I want out. I am so unhappy and he is such a selfish man.'

I said to her, 'Lady, you are talking to the wrong person here if you think I am going to buy into anything you say. As a medium psychic I look for the truth and sense the truth, not what is right or wrong, but what is actually unfolding.'

Then she asked me, 'Will I be happy with this new man?'

So I answered her saying, 'Well, I take love and personal relationships very seriously and I will not give you any excuses to justify your belief in actions that will cause other people suffering.'

Then I explained to her, 'I see things differently and I am going to be very hard on you but only because in my heart there is a great kindness from Spirit, an understanding and a grace that sees through all of this that is going on around you.' Then I asked her, 'Do you really believe that these statements you have made about your husband are true?'

With great conviction she said, 'Yes he is a boring twit, he watches eight hours of TV a day and I want to leave.'

'OK,' I said, 'well it is time for you to take a walk down the truthful road for I don't feel he is a bad man at all. If I thought he was then I would tell you to run girl but I don't feel he is at all. Let's cut through all this emotional belief if you want to know the truth. So I am going to ask you some questions. Do you absolutely believe that your husband is a boring twit? This is your label for him. Is that really, really true? Answer me honestly.'

She said, 'Yes, that is the truth.'

Again I asked her, 'Is it true in your heart that he watches eight hours of TV a day. Is that true?'

And again with great conviction she said, 'Yes that is true.'

So I said, 'Do you honestly believe your thoughts are true?'

She answered, 'Yes without doubt.'

'Right,' I said, 'this is the day we start talking truth. As I said, I don't believe your husband is a bad man or a boring twit and that comes from Spirit and from me too. Since you have known him for over twenty years has he always been a boring twit?'

'No,' she said 'for the first ten years he was there for me and for our daughters. He loved us, worked hard and used to take us out for picnics and walks in the park. He was a very loving and attentive man who was very much for his family.'

So I said, 'The truth is then that he is not in absolute fact your boring twit. It isn't true.'

Then I said to her, 'That is what he has become in your belief of him. Let's look at your second truth which is that he is watching eight hours of TV every day. I don't think any man watches eight hours of TV a day. In common sense not even a film or TV critic would watch that much a day. And yet you believe that to be true. OK, honestly in reality, how many hours does he actually watch a day.'

'OK,' she said, 'he watches about two hours a day.'

The whole audience sighed and some chuckled.

I told her, 'I will tell you what I think. I bet you tell him how stupid his is, how he is not a real man, how he does not live up to your expectations, how he is inconsiderate and does not talk to you anymore. Basically every day you tell him how rubbish he is.'

'Too right,' she said 'that is what he is!'

I replied, 'This is not about him. That could be Mr Blobby there sitting watching the TV. That could be any man because this is not about him. I believe he loves you very much and your daughters.'

She answered me saying, 'He never shows it anymore!'

I said to her, 'Look at it this way. If someone told you every day that you were rubbish, that you were not a real woman and you could never fulfil their expectations then what would you do? Your arm would reach out and you would press the button on the telly and you would get lost in the TV because that would be something you had control over that would take you away from the misery.'

Then I continued, saying to her, 'This is about you girl. It sounds like I am being harsh on you and cornering you but I am doing this out of the greatest compassion in my heart. I don't want to see you suffer any more.'

I asked her, 'Does that make sense to you so far? '

She replied, 'Kind of but I have still had enough of him and what he is like.'

Then I answered her, 'One of Judgement's best friend is called labelling. So let's get to the core of this and what this is all about because I am going to help you today. And I want you to answer me honestly. It is not what you think he is, it is how you feel when you have those thoughts.'

Then I continued, 'As I said he could be anyone sitting there watching the telly so answer me this. How does it make you feel when you see him sitting there watching the telly? Tell me what your feelings are.'

Her answer was, 'I feel alone and not wanted or valued, like I don't even exist. I feel like he doesn't care for the children and I feel pushed out and not loved.'

I asked her, 'Do you think he did all that?'

'Yes,' she said.

I said to her, 'No he hasn't. That is how you interpret the situation that you created.'

Her answer was, 'No I don't. I am always there caring for him.'

So I said, 'It sounds like you are defending your beliefs here and your judgements. Just bide with me a little bit longer and we will find an answer here. Let's go back to your childhood, when you were 6 or 7 or 8 maybe, no older than that. I feel your relationship with your parents was very difficult especially with your father.'

She answered me saying, 'Yes.'

Then I asked her, 'How did that make you feel?'

She said, 'Although they looked after me they were not loving at all and they preferred my older sister to me.'

She continued, 'They were always telling me I was not good enough. I felt pushed out, unloved and alone. I felt I wasn't valued at all.'

I said, 'Thank you for being honest with me. This is where the answer lies. If you can imagine having those emotional experiences as a 6 or 7 year old and not being able to make sense of them because you have no point of reference or judgement. You are just deeply uncomfortable with them and can't even understand why and so that sits in your emotional psyche and then becomes your hidden yardstick. Now let's move forty years into the future. Have not all your relationships been similar? The two relationships before you married your husband?'

'Yes,' she said 'they all let me down.'

I continued, 'So, from this sense of hidden fear of not being loved, of being abandoned and alone, you have compensated for that in your life. I can see that you are a business woman.'

She said, 'Yes. I have two little businesses going.'

So I told her, 'Your businesses are your proof that you are right because you are successful and it is a power and an independence that you have control over. You have compensated for this unfinished business of childhood sadness which was dumped on you and it is not even you.'

Then I said to her, 'You are innocent but it has unknowingly been the hidden secret within you. As you go through life it is like you are still looking for approval from the parents who were supposed to love you but who would kick you down. Isn't that the pattern in your relationships? You have become a self-fulfilling prophecy of your own unknowingly manufacturing through judgement and recreating this empty unknown experience. Just trying to make sense of it through the person you love. Then you will turn on them and tell them what is wrong with them, what they should do, how unworthy they are and how they don't fulfil your expectations.'

Then I added, 'Just like your parents did to you. And did you know your parents were told the same story?

You have learnt to be very strong mentally because of it but emotionally you are very insecure in your relationships. Can you see how all of this unfinished business of childhood sadness has been weaving its way through in all the relationships you have whether it is work, personal or family.'

I carried on and said to her, 'I am going to tell you this. Your husband loves you very much and the children. And your old boyfriend on the side he is from school. Isn't that right? He is not the same person that you loved as a child and as a teenager. Spirit tells me to tell you to do this. For the next week, while you are at home, you do not judge your husband. You do not pick fault or disempower him in any way. You just let him be. Then you will call me after one week and I will give the answer which is the best direction to go.'

Anyway just over a week later she phoned me and she said, 'You won't believe what's happened! I didn't have any bad thoughts about him, I just got on with my life and I was even friendly. After about three days he sat me down and turned the telly off and told me how much he still loves me and loves the children but it was hard for him to find a way to show that love because he felt so pushed out,' then she said to me, 'and he didn't put the TV on for the rest of the week. He took me and the girls out for walks and for dinner. He even took me out to a place where we used to go when we first got together and had a picnic, just like old times.'

She continued saying, 'When we were at the picnic I could see in his eyes that love and do you know, deep down, when I wasn't judging him I realised that I still loved him too.'

Then she told me, 'Anyway on the Friday my best friend phoned me and said she had seen this other man Andrew out and told me he has another two girlfriends on the go and has a reputation as a bit of a womaniser.'

She said, 'I realised then that all I was doing was running away from my own fears and I still loved my husband and the other man was history from that moment. I still loved my husband but I had stopped valuing him because of my own conditional love. I know the answer now and I know which way to go. I am staying with my husband.'

She said to me, 'By the way Rudi, this has been a great freeing for me on the deepest levels,' and then she asked me, 'What was the answer you were going to tell me about which way to go?'

And I said to her, 'To go with the calling of your Spirit, your Heart and not with the judgement of your Mind.'

I have given you two stories here, one from my own journey and one from someone else's. They are not to show who is to blame but to show how all of us play our parts in forming relationships. Innocently that then become our emotional codependent suffering and fear based identity in the search of Love.

This relates to an old saying, ' Give me a child until the age of seven and I will give you the man,' which is saying we fill our children with the Love that we have or the Love that we have lost and that child will continue the story in its own unique way but it is always Love's betrayal. We don't need to teach our children how to Love or what Love is because they already know.

ILLNESS

Ok. The world is full of healers of every denomination, whether Spiritual or medical. They are there to fix our problems. Everyone has got answers to do it this way or that way because they know best. I have been to hundreds of psychic shows and sat and talked with psychologists and doctors and all I see is the sick healing the sick.

Everybody wants to be healed of their sicknesses whether physical, mental or emotional. We all want to be healed of these Mind made diseases. Illness always comes after the event of the cause. Even if you get knocked down by a car this was caused by the Mind because in some way you put yourself in the right place at the right time and so did the driver of the car. You were both fulfilling the unfinished business of childhood sadness or should I say shared energetic belief. Like attracts like. The sadness is also the energetic shock from the first lie of Judgement taking control of your Spirit or should I say making you forget the Love that your Spirit is.

The hidden fear is born upon the betrayal of our innocence in the realisation and unremembered disappointment of being born into an impermanent mortal world. It flares up when we can't rationalise the bombardment of Mind's beliefs and also when inner freedom has had enough of being imprisoned.

All illness is the lies we hide from the truth of what we are. What I am really trying to say here is that something is broken in us in childhood that then resonates through our whole lives trying to fix itself through the drama of life. If you can imagine that as a child you are born free, a free Spirit, into an organic body and a Mind of survival and protection and you can't have survival or protection without the duality of Judgement. There is a sickness in us all. It is a fear that is imbedded in our childhood as we grow, a fear born in the realisation and unknowing separation from the Love that we are.

It is a fear that implants itself in such a way it hides itself in survival's desires which then becomes the hidden template of how we govern our lives. As an innocent Spirit, as a child who is awake and aware, we suddenly get betrayed and told to believe in things that are not true. That hurt is like a punch to the Spirit and an attack upon innocence. And the attacker of innocence then tells us the hurt we feel is just our imagination.

## THE MIND IS DEATH

All illnesses are created by the Mind that you believe yourself to be. It is the lie that it is, that is your illness. By only being absolutely aware of your Mind's damage that it causes your body in the physical film drama of your life story then you will become ill. This can be either singularly or as a collective belief structure. It is your Mind that is your illness. Your Spirit is always well and creating life.

The drama of your Mind is your suffering, your hidden secrets, your ego and it is your God of Judgement until Judgement Day comes on your death. That is why knowing your death for real is a great leveller, not only for you but for the observers of your death. The bullshit stops. The Mind has done its job carrying your coffin grinning at your funeral and then forgets you once you are burnt or buried.

Those who know their Spirit and who they are as Spirit can never die. Only the Mind's body dies. The Mind is the illness in its story. The Mind is death. It knows death and fears it absolutely. So it creates your story, your life, who you think you are and the whole Mind thing is your illness. By believing your Mind you believe you are going to die but the Mind in itself knows whatever it lives through can't die.

The Mind can only know itself as it walks grinning alongside your coffin knowing it killed the physical form through the lie and the drama it proved to be true.

But ultimately they both, Mind and Body, did not know your Spirit allowed them both to live through Spirit itself.

## ANGER

Anger has a point. Anger is an energy and it is how we understand it and what we do with it that is so important. I don't want to be a liberal limp pacifist because liberalism is the festering ground for the emotional fuse of anger. We have to be able to discern between Mind's emotional anger which is extremely destructive and simple reactive short-lived anger which is instinctive. In the wake of emotional anger the ripples that pour out of it can resonate far and deep then returning back to itself and damaging the host it came from.

Anger comes from frustration and fear. Frustration anger is different from fear anger or the anger of freedom that lifts you up out of suppression but not in retribution. That is anger used wisely but all anger leads to destruction. When we use anger to supress others then that is our Mind's emotional anger which is the unfinished business of hidden fears.

Which anger eats away at you? Don't you just hate your Mind? Anger is like a fuse which burns very quickly or slowly but launches the rocket of freedom and redemption or the rocket of destruction and imprisonment. Is it a smouldering fuse or a fast burning fuse? Anger can trigger action and it can trigger destruction. This is why I say we all have to catch ourselves when angry to discern what type of anger it is in awareness before we light that fuse.

I am writing about this because it is important and it affects everybody's lives and we need some form of understanding of what we feel when anger raises its energetic wanting. Does it serve peace or turmoil? We have to be very clear in seeing how the action we take from emotional anger resonates long term in ourselves first, then in our communities and then in our nations. I am focussing not on instinctive anger but on the big beast emotional anger. Mind's emotional anger eats away at you and twists you on the inside and turns you violent. When your Spirit observes anger it just says, 'Why? When the Spirit says, 'Why?' it is not because it does not know why, it is asking you, your Mind and by saying, 'Why are you being angry?' in awareness it releases it, knowing that its power is only in its story which isn't true. Anger is a force and it is what you do with it that matters Anger is like a bomb going off, it will cause destruction every time even if it appears to be for the good. It just depends how big your bomb is. Jesus turned over the tables in the temple so even he got angry. There is nothing wrong with anger as long as you know what it is as an expressive energy.

All this creates negative energy because at no point has there been a silent witness or awareness to let honesty of Spirit talk through us because the majority of us do not believe we have a Spirit. If you don't believe you have a Spirit you can never see anger for what it is and be aware of all that happens around it. Your Spirit is God within that does not know anger and can never get angry. Only Mind's God gets angry.

The anger is the betrayal that you have been shown in childhood and life's journey that you could never understand in unsaid cruelty which is the anger that is always there etched so deep within, laying unconsciously dormant until it is triggered by jealousy, blame, revenge and imprisonment. These are just some of the aspects it uses to shape and mould you to feed itself.

Anger itself is another energetic energy that we use in creating Soul personality because deep beneath the energy of anger is the Love that you want but have not found or can't see. Anger itself, if you can imagine, is like a beast that feeds on the energy of anger which is born from your fear of separation from the Love that you are and the Mind's love that you chase.

Spirit does not have anger. The nearest that Spirit gets to anger is passion. Passion is the energetic power of the God within you, which is not anger based, shouting out or motivating action freeing the innocent.

Isn't it strange how at first, just for a moment, when people say, 'Forgive them for they know not what they do,' the Mind presents this bag of feelings of anger saying, 'Forgive them! How? Why should I after what they have done to me?' and in that thought there is a rising of energetic pay back.

This is your arrogant Mind vindicating itself but then the quiet voice within you says, 'Forgive them for they don't know what they do,' which really means you should be saying to yourself, 'I am still angry because I have to forgive myself for I don't know what I do.'

This is not easy because anger is an energy that proves existence. When we can't have Love's energy we pursue anger's energy in its false interpretation of love. Real innocent Love disarms anger. Anger is where Love is misunderstood or taken away.

# CHAPTER 13

# THE FEELING UNIVERSE

If we are all one consciousness, if we are that which manifests the whole universe, then why do we exist? I feel that Oneness did not know itself. It knew everything but how could Oneness separate itself into individualised consciousness in Oneness to know itself? It's impossible! So consciousness had to divide itself somehow so it could feel itself.

ONENESS KNOWING ITSELF

Remember feelings that I spoke about?

Consciousness became a feeling universe and the universe exploded into existence in the immensity of the force of feeling as the universe divided into existence. Some people call it the big bang theory. How awesome is that? It succeeded and exploded into a billion trillion stars and more. And like the smallest atom a star had a planet going around it with blue nitrogen skies and oceans and then the first scream of human birth coming into this world! Holy shit I'm here!

What would you make if you were Oneness to feel and know yourself, not to know it but to feel it? (We are all IT.)

You would create an organic body with an individualised conscious Spirit that animates its human form, the perfect shape for expression, and at the same time give it an organic Mind of the greatest intelligence which does not know, and will never know, that your Spirit exists as the absolute truth which lives through physical form not for Mind's purpose.

You would create a Mind and Body which absolutely does not know who it is and can only find its freedom and know itself through the energy of Love's feeling that is transformed by Mind and Body into the magnificent story of consciousness to consciousness in division not separation.

The word, 'Why?' is to give reason to things called feelings and all feelings are Love in disguise, Love disguised in Mind's eye. Mind can only become the archetype that opens the doorway to seeing who you really are. We are all Oneness in the absolute magnificence of feeling of individuality. We are all Eternal Spirit for ever living absolute reality in the heart centre of Love. So get your flipping head round that one!

How can you find the knowledge and intellect that you already are? That is in the peace that you are within.

Your Mind is like a finger trying to work out how the Body exists. It is a finger and that is it. The vastness within you in its silent voice or voiceless Spirit already knows why everything is. If you ask your finger it can't work it out. It is a bit like this.

We have all these amazing scientists working on the theories of the universe, of space and quantum mechanics. We have all these physicists, chemists and mathematicians all looking for the source of who we are and looking for some intelligence. They are all trying to find out how, from nothing, the universe evolved but they are looking for an intelligent creator or a consciousness that is made up of a God particle that is quantifiable and measurable as something separate that can only be understood in the duality Mind of separation. Science is duality looking for answers.

My belief is that Consciousness is not made of a particle, only its after movement will be observed as energy in motion, that might be called a God particle, that is the forming of the etheric templates of any size for matter to exist and form in.

If we just stop there and freeze for a second.

It is the searching consciousness within these people that is slapping them in the face and saying, 'I am here in you duh! I am the reason and the answer duh! Don't you get it?' but they would all rather be a finger looking for the body it grows on. All of them looking and looking and looking with this wondrous consciousness within them, asking the peace within themselves, 'What is the truth?'

It is like the answer is already here. You are the answer that speaks and you are the absolute pinnacle of creation. This whole universe which we created for us to know itself is the vastness of who you are. You are not anything at all. You are this peace that is within you and sits here and at the end of the universe all at the same time in this very moment. When you are in peace your little stupid Mind with all its drama and fear does not make sense anymore. How can it?

When the silent voice of the Love within you, that you are, holds you in its embrace of who you are then you are already home. Already home every second of every day but you just don't know it or believe it.

I think somewhere it says in the Bible,

*'The foxes have holes, and the birds of the air have nests; but the Son of man hath nowhere to lay his head.'*

The sons of God have nowhere to rest their heads or sleep for we humans never seem to find that peace anywhere because the whole universe is our home.

## THE WORTHY ADVERSARY

Isn't it strange that sometimes you can be talking away to people and being animated with your facts and your proofs which have been repeated so many times that they just run off your tongue in a bizarre twisted need of being in control?

It is like the Mind is chattering away out of your control, playing the recording and there is a voice within you saying,

'That is not who I am. That is not even true what I am saying.' It is almost like the Mind's story has become a shield to hide or protect your Spirit but in fact it is imprisoning your Spirit. It imprisons your Spirit because this is a strange contract between Judgement and your Spirit, your consciousness.

Almost like saying, 'Do whatever you can Judgement, paint whatever story, have whatever belief, suffering, pain, even death. Do your very, very best to see if you can stop consciousness, to stop Spirit shining through because the harder you make it the stronger I become.' It is almost like consciousness has a self-fulfilling prophecy in its wanting to be aware of itself. Your Mind has to be a worthy adversary for consciousness to know itself and even so big it would create universes.

Consciousness knows though that it has already won because it is its own battle. It is absolute Love testing itself. This is the power of consciousness not material power dancing out its game in form.

GOD IN DISGUISE

What if the mystery is this, that your Spirit is not made of matter and not made of elements because it was before elements? What if this thing that you are is the whole universe in you aware of itself?

What if we are all God in disguise? We are magnificence in human form but not made of elements. All life lives through us and is created because of us, US without a Mind, US the ultimate secret, never owned, never known but absolutely everywhere. You cannot hide from the truth that you are. The silent witness within that moves the stars and fires the guns, gives birth to nations and death to the starving.

You are all these things. You cannot hide for long from who you truly are. We are all sparks of the absolute divine consciousness of the universe only to be felt through Mind's dream.

It is very scary to even contemplate for a second that this is who you are in the judgement Mind, but you know, as you think it, there is a pulling and a gentle absolute knowing that you are more than your sum total. You are the unspoken voice that talks through everything and is everything all reflected in the mirror of your created Soul. Once broken by death only Spirit is eternal.

Upon this knowing and having this thought, I still see an old lady catching the bus in the rain with her wrinkled face and hopeful eyes of a world that was never seen.

She had forgotten that she was a child of God, shaped in Mind's emotional dream, catching the bus and kind of knowing, without knowing, this whole experience is eternity unfolding forever. Just there, getting by, getting through. This old lady is life's longing to be lived through all things and did any of this even matter in the end? Then a baby takes its first breath and its first cry and it all starts again.

We spend our life looking for certainty, creating certainties in all that we do, not knowing or believing that we are the uncertainty which will never stay still in life's longing to breathe. The only certainty is known and seen in the absolute silent stillness. That is where you will find your certainty for ever.

## WHAT HOLDS MY BODY TOGETHER?

I just had another strange thought.

What holds my body together? And this room? And this house? What holds my physical body in this shape together? Why doesn't it just fall to bits?

How does it know to have this shape when really everything is just a bunch of atoms flying around at different speeds creating shapes out of its atomic structures and all being energy forming structure? What is this invisible force or thing that holds it all together? We have this body that we take for granted and in it we have this Mind that thinks. We have this feeling of existence but who is feeling the existence? What is this invisible thing that I am aware of, and you are aware of, that is almost like observing you but also is you.

This amazing force is not of elements or matter. It has no form. It is just always here. It feels like an invisible everything that has become separate in a thing called Body. This consciousness, or we can call it Spirit, was here before we were born and is here now and will be here after we have gone. And when I say we I mean me, myself and I, my Mind identity.

We are this magnificent life that runs through everything and is conscious of everything forming shape for emotional expression. Our human shape is perfect for this. It is the etheric expression that moulds the shape of all that is and the human being that our Spirit dances in.

## ETHERIC TEMPLATE OF CONSCIOUSNESS

The etheric is consciousness templates formed out of resonance formed from a singularity of resonance. It is string theory. Each string is every form from atoms to humans to worlds to stars to galaxies to universes to the beginning and ending. It is etheric shaping which matter then presents itself through in temporal time.

When we die we are not born again in physical form. In the Biblical stories it says one day we will resurrect from the dirt on redemption day and be whole again in our form which is the same body anew. It is not true. What we really are is this unimaginable, unthinkable mystery of magnificence that is born into the seeds of matter, that grows into a flower or a human that is born and will die. Our form is born into an etheric template of consciousness will, but what is born is eternal and has never been born and can never die. This is the eternal truth. We are life's longing and once born into matter it becomes free, even though its host dies and the host itself is absolutely beautiful and perfect in its so called imperfection.

We are consciousness that has to be born through separation. That is the only way consciousness is aware of itself as a separate spark lit up by the sum of all existence. We are the Angels of life's longing to express Love.

## HOLDING THE FIRE WITHIN

I feel like I am going mad being torn between knowing I am the one that is nothing that lives through me (some would call it the Tao) but then with my eyes and form I live in a world full of Mind's dreams created and held together through the God of separation, or should I say duality, which is the protecting and survival force for physical form and experience that lives in time called Judgement.

How can I hold the fire within that is always free and alive?

It is empowered by this endless universal energy called consciousness which is fearless and noble and free and full of joy in the present moment. Like a gift of life, the present of life itself, it is here but there is something so deeply embedded, like a wall of fear or resistance, that is so afraid to let go.

For you to be able to walk in your living Spirit and form you have to die metaphorically alive or die literally and absolutely to know this.

You would think by being aware of this absolute truth of something within you that is untouchable that somehow you would become all 'love and light' and nothing could hurt you. Although on one level you are free the more you become aware in silent holy witness there is another level on which you are far more open to seeing the world is full of walking liars. Not in judgement or blame but with an uncomfortable revelation that mankind lives in lies, killing honesty and truth and making us look away and not even recognise our Spirit within. I too was once a walking liar, not because I am a liar but because what I believed was the lie.

The majority of people only take on board information that reinforces their lie, as a fact, as proof, protecting this invisible thing, this power, which the Mind thinks itself to be. It becomes its own lie because it doesn't know the invisible thing which is the Spirit you that the Body, Mind and Soul are born through and live through but can never know or understand. In so doing it produces your

Soul personality which is not who you are because your Spirit can never have a personality.

How can you relate to a world which wants you to believe in a lie of desire and need and want when in your Spirit you are saying,

'This is uncomfortable. I don't need anything. I am already free and happy and this is my beautiful world. My Spirit with everyone else's Spirit created this world, our Garden of Eden. Consciousness called our Spirit to live upon Mother Earth where everything is given to us so that living consciousness can exist in form and eat, walk, look, talk, taste and feel through Spirit. The Earth is our gift to ourselves as living proof of the vastness and wonderful Love that we are.

Everything that man builds from a duality Mind, like cars and houses, is like a cancer which grows and grows until eventually it will kill its host. Another example of this cancer is born out of the emotional judgemental Mind of men which then turns us into walking liars that imprison our Spirit for it can never know the truth that we are.'

Has the penny dropped yet that you are not your goddamn Mind that is born out of suffering and survival? I am not being liberal or conceptual here. Do you get it? Honesty leads us to the truth and the truth leads us to freedom and freedom lets us know who we truly are as loving God in disguise.

## THE ROLLER COASTER OF THE MIND

When we are still without thinking, just being, just here, then we start to feel alive without even trying. We feel comfortable, well and safe as if some massive unknowing tiny but immense energy wants to fall into us but the moment we begin to grow in that then suddenly this wall of the Mind filters it into understanding and the connection is broken. We are off into the future and the past and our thoughts of acquiring and surviving again defining ourselves through fear based belief.

When will this insane roller coaster stop? But thinking of the roller coaster is the Mind again assimilating me relentlessly into belief. Well the answer is,

'Just don't go there. Give it back to the invisible. Trust the unknown and the unseen just for a moment.'

The unseen is like the Earth, moon and stars, the sun and the ocean, all living things and they have never asked of you anything, not once, but give without question so your body can live. Then the ugly Mind always wants more. It wants to acquire, to destroy what it doesn't like, to hold onto what it does like, all in its separateness of actually believing that everything is separate, even fellow human beings. All is to be oppressed and controlled in the suffering Mind holding itself in emotional identity of its own personal form of conceit which is the enemy of the truth. My Mind is the voice which always talks of me, myself and I, a trinity of imprisonment.

I just want to live alive, free in the love that I am in the world that I love with the humanity I love, not in the cruel lie of the Mind. Damn I have got some serious habituated patterns here! But behind those patterns of thought and doing there is a living dancing Spirit that smiles with the reason of the absolute knowing like a smile that wraps around my head three times because it is so damn good. I think it is called loving freedom. That is who we are. I keep doing my best to run away from it, even believing that it is not true but it is a bit like you can run and you run but you just die tired because you will be free sooner or later. Which one do you choose?

When you say the words in your Mind,

'I choose to be free,' you can almost hear the Demon of Judgement open up its wings and shout out,

'Freedom! What?'

Then my Spirit just smiles and giggles. Can you see it? Can you feel this silent you agreeing but with a refreshing energy because the world appears, or should I say looks, different even though it is the same old world.

It is a very strange place when you come to the point where I am right now writing this book, where everything I had or owned or thought I owned or believed in has gone. But as it goes I can't go back there and my Mind in the freedom of truth has no roads for the future. As I say that I can feel the dark Mind reaching up to grasp me and find answers and new controls and new beliefs and new pretend ways but then in my Spirit I say, 'No. Go. Let go,' and as I say that then up shoot the hooks of unknown fear to reel me back down into a profoundly sick society of people asleep in their Mind's dream.

It is not even as if I want to reach up to a higher light, I just want to be free of all the goo and the shackles of the theatre of life or should I say the dramatic theatre of life. Just let it go and everything is alright.

There is no wanting in being here and now but there is living and being in the here and now for your Body is your home and the garden is your world, all being walked gently in Spirit. But will that world sustain me?

Freedom is God's manna. Did your Mind ever give you anything that is forever?

The more you let go, bizarrely, the more you have and then your Mind jumps around like a crazed monkey, an old friend screaming and shouting. It can't bear to accept that you are going to release it and be free because it knew you were always free until the monkey demon jumped on your back. The monkey demon was pulled out of the bag of sin as a child from the bag being held by your mum, your dad, your culture and your country.

Greed, tradition and religion. You had no chance.

The world will beat you down whether through glory or destruction but when you are on the floor and the dirt is in your nostrils and your tongue is dry and your eyes can't cry any more then strangely the story ends. It is like you have run out of words, you have given up, only to release yourself into the one thing that has never given up, the real you.

BURIED IN THE DEEPEST MINE

If I was buried in the deepest of deepest mines ten miles down in the darkness where my nose touched the roof and my arms couldn't move in the darkest place knowing for sure that I would die and no one could hear my screams, I know what holds me trapped in this deepest of mines is the world of the Mind which will kill me physically, mentally and emotionally. And I know absolutely the moment I let go I will open my eyes in paradise, free for eternity, where I was all the time but I just had to awake from Mind's dream which I believed to be true. And so can you right now. It is called courage and living fearlessly.

Now it is time to do the household chores and iron my son's clothes, because he has got to go to school tomorrow, and tidy up the house.

Do you get it?

## LIFE'S LONGING TO TELL ITS STORY

All the words I speak that have been given to me and I use to describe my journey, all these words are momentary words eclectically put together so God's voice can talk to your emotional looking.

It is like life's longing waiting to tell its story with the words of experience from the library of words built up along the way which inspired me. Those kinds of words that make you go, 'Oh wow! That's good,' or made me laugh or should I say made me be aware that there was something more in me that they resonated with.

It is funny how they all fall together over the years into the story of words saying words that can't be said or written. This book is not about you becoming positive which in itself is another lie. It is about giving you permission to be human with living Spirit in you, to be an ambassador of your Spirit, not as an ego but as a human being.

Your frailty is God calling out from you. The fear and suffering always waits on the edge of the cliff when you only have to take one more step into freedom. When you do take that step you don't fall off the cliff because there is a land beyond the veil that has always been there. It is called you.

Dare you take that blind step without security or promises?

# CHAPTER 14

# LIFE FORCE

Where does the life force come from? We are life and it runs through us and it is there but we can't see it but everything exists through it. Even when we look into ourselves we are alive. There is something animating us, this invisible force which scientists look for and can't find. They know of energy but they can't find this life force itself that actually holds the whole universe together, that IS the universe. In a strange way you are that life force that is living and that is in everything, even in your Body and your Mind.

That is what this force lives through but the Mind never looks to its life force that actually gives it life because it doesn't know how. All of us want to feel this great sense of life that empowers us but we don't know how to find it or look for it and we ask, 'Does it exist anyway?' but it is still there. It is hard to even imagine that what we really pursue is to be as one with this life force that we are because we only ever feel it in brief moments in this life through certain emotional experiences. It is always here and always in you. You can't put your finger on it but it is here, right now, right this second.

The moment you relax your Mind just to be aware of it, your Mind starts going into a spin and tries to find some anchor or point of reference to understand its value to us, to you, as a Mind. That is the Mind trying to beat consciousness and to be stand-alone consciousness. It is just here always.

You can't grab it and you can't hold it or see it as a thing. It is everything and everything lives through it. You are the everything and everything lives through you, your body and your form. Your sense of being alive, feeling alive right now, that lifefulness of you is who you are. That is the secret. You are what can never be named and is nothing at all and is everything that is at the same time. Sounds a bit like God eh?

## LETTING GO OF MIND

How can you ignore the life that you are? Aliveness is who you are and the whole universe. Awake this second. You can't find and look for what you are because you are already here. This is it. The madness is looking for it. Do you get it? Don't you dare think and go back to sleep!

Knowing this is not going to turn you into some enlightened guru. Only your Mind can do that. What it screams out is living. Live your life! Live it! When I say live your life that is not just go and party, although you can do that if you wish, it is loving living your own Spirit. But how can you live your own Spirit when it attaches itself to everything and there is no point of reference? How can the nothing that is everything have a point of reference? But this is who you are.

If you let yourself go into that by being still then your Mind desperately follows its own point of reference to habitually latch onto an emotional story and pull you back into believing that you are separate from all things.

Actually, let's just stop there.

This is all floating with Angels stuff in a way.

It is floating around with words which sound nice and wise but how does this work practically in our so called normal daily lives? Can you imagine the factory worker as he clocks in saying to his mates,

'By the way chaps, I am One,' or, 'Hey boss I am One with everything.'

In their Minds he would have just lost the plot and would rapidly go down the evolutionary scale of their belief system, mad as a fruitcake or, 'What the hell has he been drinking or taking?'

How on earth in these two extremes can anyone trust you or believe that you are something more than what appears to be?

So what happens is we give in to the greater will which is the Mind's judgement and join the herd again. This is the one thing that will keep dragging you down and bringing you back into the habituated regularity, conformity and dependency of Mind's group belief. It does drive you mad and gets quite frustrating, not because you want to fix or save anyone but just because you know that what they believe to be isn't true and what they believe with the judgement Mind is everything they don't want in their lives.

We all have moments where we do things and we feel great. It can be sports, going out or just getting out there but the next day you have to put your head down like a troglodyte and go back into the system, go back into the machine that holds you for forty to seventy hours or more a week just to have the money to break free for a moment and then you die. How mad is that?

It is not about being a rebel it is about really knowing that we can create a better world; a world with loving purpose and not a world with demanding wanting of power at any cost to human dignity.

What I am trying to say here is that we are all more than this. We are all more than the stories and the dramas and the needs and the wants. We are eternal Spirits living but you cannot see it and will never see it until you stop looking. He who can be perfectly still will become the truth and the light.

When I say still I mean still in the very present moment with no wanting, no action, no freezing up and no thinking but just aware and awake. What appears is this vastness of what you are as an eternal son of the universe, or should I say shining sun of the universe, that is always here and always has been and always will be whether you like it or not. Do you get it?

You can never get inspired or do anything without knowing who you truly are or while you are in the mind-set of the Mind endlessly trying to manifest this great Spirituality through a false Mind's constructed belief which comes from the same Mind that imprisons you. But we do it because everything has to be filtered through the Mind.

The truth is you choose to filter everything through your Mind because you still believe that you are your Mind. Your Mind believes that is you and resistance again is futile in Mind's dream. When you let go of the Mind that identifies you, you will find there is a spiritual intelligent Mind that is aware of all things and has always been there.

## JUMPING THE SHIP

The only way is to side step it without any reason. It is like jumping the ship for no reason.

You just do it. Even though you have been told stories that when you jump the ship you will fall into the sea that will freeze you and finally drown you.

The ship is full of people on it. You can imagine us all on ships, hundreds of ships, out at sea on this rough ocean. We are all sailing to this Promised Land, setting the compass bearing of our dreams and all going there although we are not quite sure exactly where it is. And we all look at each other on the ships and get to know each other as friends and as enemies but no one will dare jump the ship because they will drown in the ocean and there is nowhere to go. It is safe on the ship, you have all that you need and all the boats are going in the same direction to this Promised Land but no one questions the Captain of the ship.

If you did he would just say, 'They are the rules. That is where we are going,' but did you know if you jump the ship and you fall into the vast ocean you don't die. The ocean that you float around in turns into solid ground with the sun shining and when you look from your beach you see the ships sailing off into the distance knowing that all of the people on the boat think that you have drowned.

What I am trying to say is, 'Jump the ship of your Mind,' but just know that you are not going back and there is the rub. Do you or don't you?

This is the God within you saying, 'I dare you,' and in those words God is saying, **'Truth is a one way ticket to freedom.'** Stop waiting for some God to grab you and wipe your sins free or to heal you or inspire you so you can live once that has happened.

The truth is that has never happened to anyone since the dawn of man. The God of liberation only gives you that when you let go of the God of the Mind that imprisons you. The moment you do that then you will become free.

Sounds good but dare you try it? You have got to catch every moment that you run for freedom. Kick open the gates and you will hear and sense the master of the Mind that watches you like a hawk turn its head and say, 'What the hell do you think you are doing? Where are you going?'

Every moment you have a sense or a feeling of liberation of Spirit the Rottweiler of the Mind turns its head and growls at you. You know it but you are so scared you give in and go back to the pack.

But who is it that gives in? Who is it that reasons with you? That is the last person you have to let go of and it is called Judgement again. It is your habituated persona of identity. So just stop.

The power is catching yourself. As I said earlier, 'Who is talking? and whoever talks is not who you are. When you know that with such passion, with such love of your Spirit, then you are free. Free to live.

## YOUR MIND IS YOUR ABUSIVE PARTNER

Your Mind is your abusive partner. Once you threaten to leave it will beg you, it will do whatever it can to hold onto you and you usually give in and all is well for a little bit but then the same abuser has just changed its tactics, but the abuser itself is also the abused. That is why you forgive them but even in that liberal understanding is your abuser within your head, your Mind, cleverly imprisoning you and robbing you of your life and, in a strange way, you like it because it is a story, a drama. Whether it is beautiful or ugly, it is your story and drama, your believed identity.

The moment you leave your Mind it turns its demonic head and turns and looks at you and says,

'What do you think you are doing? Where are you going? Who do you think you are? Just stop. Don't go anywhere. How can you leave after all the things I have done for you and given you? I have always been there for you. I protected you. And this is how you repay me. You selfish ungrateful Soul! Was I not there when you were the happiest? Was I not there when you were in your darkest place and suffering? I was always with you and now you have got the audacity to go. You don't know where you are going anyway. Tell me and I might have some ideas if you don't know.

Have you lost your tongue now? Can't you talk to me? Are you ignoring me? Who the hell do you think you are? If you loved me you would stay and I would love you back again.

Where are you going? Don't jump into the sea because you will be alone. You don't need anyone but me. Look at all the things I have done for you. I know who you truly are. Don't I keep your secrets? Don't I protect you? And now you want to leave. You don't even have a good reason.

Stop pretending to be standing still because your feet are shifting slowly like you are about to jump off my ship. I promise I will make your life better if you don't go but if you insist on going I will tell everybody on this ship what a loser you are. Just like all the others who have jumped the ship.'

So just bloody jump the ship! Do you get it?

## LOVE AND LIGHT WORKERS

I have just been on Facebook watching the Spiritual banter of the healers and 'love and light workers'. They are constantly throwing at each other wonderful quotations and uplifting words with pretty pictures and at the same time they are telling each other how they need to be focused on this to be in control and how they need to be aware of this and that.

All of them are giving each other this wisdom and common sense and positive way of thinking and telling each other how to save and help themselves.

They share the advice with each other but do they understand or practice it themselves?

Are they just grabbing moments for themselves of some elitist feel good in control nonsense and then immediately sharing it with everyone else because they think they have found the Holy Grail?

But hey! This is higher Spiritual stuff which makes them feel superior to the uninformed guy in the street who doesn't know what day it is and has no purpose in life but if he did know then he would be wise and free like them. It is like they are all shouting out for help and giving help but in them there is still this massive hole of not knowing who they are.

No Spiritual wrangling or wise words or poetry of love actually breaks them out of their Mind's dream because it is the Mind that is loving all those things in this bizarre way of holding onto Mind's identity.

It is strange because these are all intelligent people who have deeply suffered and experienced life all trying to find chinks of light to hold onto from misinformed Spiritual belief.

Can't you see that this is all rubbish too? We are more beautiful than that. We are bigger and stronger than any pious or uplifting words. The words we talk and the deeds we do for any good are only fragments of the amazing unimaginable beautiful potential of what we truly are.

You must stop falling in love with the promise of these words and wisdom which are feeding you, softening you and warming your heart because it is still the same. You are just sucking off the bottle of ego and false emotional comfort of a promise of paradise. It is only killing you softly and gently holding you in the prison of your Mind for without being a living ambassador in the truth of your actions then words are just empty deeds.

Can you see that this is like an impregnable wall that people can't get over or break through?

It allows them to go so far and then stops them in the promised hope that somehow, magically, enough wise words and clever understanding will collectively (with all their spiritual Facebook friends) pull down the wall so that the love of their hearts can reach out and fully embrace what they are. In their wise words of elitist Spiritual bantering all bouncing off each other they are hoping that maybe, by magical chance, one of them will find that one thing that will break through the wall and show they were a Spiritual winner but all this is only creating Spiritually addictive behavior.

This wall can go on for ever and ever and ever because it is all of the Mind anyhow. The bricks of the wall that block them from knowing who they are, are constantly being built higher and higher and higher like a self-fulfilling prophecy of never being able to find the answer. In the questioning the bricks of the wall are constantly being formed in some heartfelt need for freedom. The wall is the Mind and it never ends. That is its job until one day we realize that we have always been Spirit and all we have got to do is step through the wall and be free because the wall does not exist. It is that simple. There is no thinking in that process.

All the words of wisdom, even the Facebook plaques and quotes, are only created in the person who has not found the love within themselves. All the words are lies crying out in the wanting to feel loved and feel safe and find something that will wash away all the fear and suffering which is so deeply embedded in the heart's disappointment of life's longing to be free. Just trying to find a place within that can never be hurt by any external suffering or conflict. Well, did you know it is already here but it can't be found or defined ever in Mind's analysis and expectation?

How can your Mind ever know the invisible because that is what it fears it most of all, like the death of itself in physical form.

BEING NICEY NICEY SPIRITUAL

I know many of you spiritual ones are thinking, 'I have got to study my chakras. I have got to study the Angels. I need to look at my purpose or find the energy and decide what is good and bad. I have got to have a community of nicey people around me. I have got to light a candle. I have got to make a prayer. I have got to be nicey nicey and Spiritual. I need to turn over my affirmation card for the day.'

Who is talking?

The clever ones among you are thinking, 'What does he know? Where is his proof? Where is his truth? He is not as clever as us. He doesn't have the 'ologies or the philosophies or all that stuff so we can't trust him.' Actually, I do have diplomas and spiritual qualifications in many fields but in reality they are all good energetic healing practices which are wonderful in themselves but none set me free.

But still it is only the TRUTH that makes you jump the ship! Do you get it? You have got to get mad at all the rubbish that runs in your head and ruins your life. Get mad this second and jump the goddamn ship!

FREEDOM OF LAUGHTER

This reminds me of one of my first parachute jumps.

There was an officer in front of me with his hands on the door doing the white knuckle job and waiting for the green light and the shout to go. His eyeballs were popping out of his head in fear and I just burst out laughing. I think they call it gallows humour!

He went out the door arms and legs spinning and I went out the door laughing with not a fear in the world because I knew once I left the door there was no going back and I kind of knew my chute would open.

Later on in the debrief the pilot said, 'Who was the first guy out the door?'

The officer answered, 'It was me.'

Then the pilot said, 'Hell I thought I had lost my propeller for a second! I give you ten out of ten for style.'

But at least we all landed safely.

Isn't it funny how in extreme moments something can suddenly be turned 180 degrees when the absurdity of fear is broken by the freedom of the laughter of your Spirit. You just know that everything is alright. Then the grim reaper will hold your hand and take you to the Beat Up Room and you are off again back into your story of worthlessness. Doesn't that just get up your nose? Like it just won't go away like some invisible predator.

The only way to stop that is to say, 'That is enough. OK predator, stand in front of me. Let's bring it on. Who the hell are you that causes me fear and disempowers me? Who are you that robs me and makes me feel worthless and talks of humiliation? Stand in front of me now! Stop all the messing about.

Just do it. In fact while I am here let's bring on all my fears and all my beliefs. Let's have my whole life's story. Let's bring it in front of me now because you are entwined in all of that too. Look me in the eye whatever you are. I don't care if you kill me. Here is your chance.'

Guess what happens? Nothing. There is nothing without the story. And in the nothing there is a silence. And deep within the nothing is peace and freedom and deeper than that is the smile of God's grace of who you are. It is so simple. Just accept it without thinking. Even if it is just for a second you have had your first taste of the freedom of who you are.

Welcome home.

## LIVING CONSCIOUSNESS

The only truth is knowing and feeling that you are living consciousness in the very present moment. You are consciously living and in that is the freedom of being alive. If you are Mind living then you are suffering. Mind living is judgement, time and fear. It pulls you away from the very present moment. It is the habituated lie. All you need to do is stop without emotionally thinking. You are living consciousness. It is a stillness that is alive and just 'is' at this very moment, absolutely aware of all that you are and all that is happening around you but it doesn't engage with the living Mind.

Your living Mind is the lesser you. It is the thief and protector of your body and life and it would feed on you and create the never ending Mind's dream of dramatised emotion which in itself plugs you into the world of everyone else who is living in their Mind. Just by stopping and feeling your consciousness living through you that is who you are. Forget any concepts of non-duality, of enlightenment and of being blissfully open because that is all Mind mumbo jumbo. You are absolutely alive living consciousness. That is who you are. Can you feel it?

## FALLING AWAKE INTO THE NOW

You can only feel it and know it. It can never be conceptualised. The moment you try conceptualising something this is your living Mind taking over with its story and identity and its Soul personality.

Your Mind, putting it bluntly, will always assimilate you into survival fear and its Mind which is judgement.

When are you going to stop the suffering? When are you going to let go? How far do you have to be beaten to the ground to wake up? How far do you have to go to enlightenment which is never truly found until boredom sets in and then you wake up? As it has been said, 'falling awake,' into the now.

I am tired of all the analytical technical mumbo jumbo although I profoundly understand it. That is for the liberal pacifists in their cynical smug narcissistic ugly realities.

You are alive. Feel it this very moment. Just feel it don't think it. The sky, the sun, the moon and the Earth and nature will affirm you are alive.

Be aware of your living consciousness that you are. That is the truth. Anything else is Mind's dream. You know this but as you think your living bullshit head keeps claiming you. You don't have to fight it you just have to honour and feel your living Spirit. And if you think anything else you are living in your head and that is why you are dead already.

Your Mind absolutely fears freedom and absolutely loves control and possession. In saying those words 'control and possession' it makes me feel sick inside and saddens my heart for I have lived my life in that place for many, many years but in my Spirit passionately waiting to be free of the stupid Mind it created to know itself. You want to fall awake willingly in every moment into your living Spirit which is right here now. It is nowhere else but right here now. If you think you have got to look for it then that is your emotional Mind talking to you. Wake up! Can't you see? You are living Spirit. That is the joy. That is the freedom. That is the love. That is God's embrace. Do you get it?

I am not going to waste your time with fancy talk because you just need to bloody wake up here and now! You are living Spirit. Stop thinking and let your living Spirit do the thinking without even thinking. Can you feel it? Then see the world anew through the eyes of your living Spirit.

Have you noticed each time you read one of my sections I am actually slapping you over and over and repeating myself in different ways on how the Mind ravages you in its tyranny? Do you get it? Brainwashing is persistent indoctrination of Mind's personalised ideals. Well I am persistently making you look at how you have been brainwashed for all these years so you can set yourself free of the imprisonment of your Mind's longing to own you in its lies.

THE INNOCENT CHILD

It is a joy to be alive and beautiful, living in life's flow, living in the now.

As a child I looked at the world in wonder filled with the richness of its taste, smells, colours, sun, moon, stars, wind and rain, everything that was never questioning but just being. Even my physical body enjoyed its ability to be a part of all things and walk with true reality.

Then somewhere in my journey I let people tell me, 'You are wrong and you are stupid. You are no good and you have failed.'

I didn't realise those were the moments that I changed without realising it. I stopped being me because I believed what they had said was true. I let go of my natural joy and love of life which was mine naturally and was always mine every second of every day. I believed from that day that I had to seek and earn life, love, joy and freedom. That day I wasn't the real me any longer because I believed I was no good anymore. I was robbed of my innocence.

With the passage of time life got hard with struggles and disappointments and then I started looking for things to blame, to blame for my failings and sadness and seeking things to give me back 'me' and redemption. Blame and guilt turned me into a coward even though I knew I was a brave warrior in my Spirit.

Something unseen had created a hidden spectre and it was like a malevolent dark ghostly force overshadowing my life. Whenever I stopped to think it was secretly telling me, 'You failed.'

After I had exhausted blaming the world I then blamed myself. I was not worthy of true love, joy, happiness or freedom and so I joined the ranks of all the other millions of people out there in the same boat lost to the ghost of the cruel seas, all passing ships in the night with the same stories of woe. I became, without much questioning, a dedicated follower of the dark shadow with many names such as worry, guilt, fear and loneliness. It robbed me of my dreams, joy and happiness and I was shackled to fear and loss.

Going back to jumping the ship, I kind of knew in my Spirit the only way out was to jump the ship (or should I say the cruise liner) into that cold and stormy sea where I would surely die. The boat I was in was filled with people just like me and we had all worked hard and been bashed and smashed by life. We were all afraid to die.

We all know that life is not always a bed of roses. In Truth, it is crueller, more unforgiving and tougher and life will knock out of you the will to live, keeping you shackled permanently until you die if you let it.

Life will ruthlessly suck from you your will to be free in its fear based relentless wanting but it is not how strongly you can fight back but knowing that only your Spirit will set you free. It is about how much you say, 'That is enough,' and believe your living Spirit is your power.

That is what will save you and set you free. It's about how much you can take and with Spirit's courage keep getting up no matter how bad it gets. Your faith can be stopped but your Spirit will never give up on you or die. It is the strength of your Spirit that makes you succeed and achieve your dreams.

At the same time you have to be willing to take the pain and struggle to make it in an uncaring world. Until you start believing in yourself you will never have a life that is truly yours, that is honouring the unique beautiful Spirit that you are! Yes you, without comparison to anything outside of yourself or negative belief inside of yourself.

It is not believing your emotional Mind's self but knowing that the self within you believes in you because it is your Holy Spirit. Just let it free and you will get up and keep getting up until you stand strong in this world again.

Your strength and courage to be you again does not sit in the Promised Land. It sits in the gentle smile in your eyes and lips filled with surety created by the simple unwavering truth of the Spirit within you.

You can feel it when you really smile with your eyes. That person behind your smiling is the good within you but you don't trust him because you would rather trust the physical world which in truth has never given you anything that is permanent. Why do we do that?

If you pursue in love and truth the nourishment of your Spirit then your actions cannot bind nor harm anyone because love and compassion cradles life's true journey which can never be bound by the hidden dark shadows of fear. They only exist in man's cowardice whose unseen army is massive but it only takes one honest voice and one true Spirit to stand in its natural humanness. This will always defeat the army of fear and control created by the words of lost Souls.

Truth is not found in wisdom or searched for. The truth we need that gives us joy, freedom and love is what we hide and run away from although it is the very thing we want. Truth and honesty walk hand in hand.

If you are not truly honest with your true self then you will become a thief and a liar and you will promise love only half true.

You will promise yourself to happiness but to be more successful you rob people of trust, you rob yourself of contentment and trust and lies give you more time to hide from the honesty. You hide in your own theft of your real beautiful self because the world of fear wears you down until you have no Soul strength left that will give you the courage to be you and sit in peace, peace which is living consciousness, consciousness living, here and now, with no shackles or story.

WE FEAR FREEDOM?

Why do we fear our freedom? The truth is we don't. It is only your Mind that fears your Spirit being free. Your Mind will then offer you its version of freedom so when you fear freedom you are only wishing to be free in Mind's dream.

My Spirit is saying, 'Do I have to shake you this second? For God's sake open up your eyes! You are here alive, awake and free. Any other thought is a lie.

I am shaking you to shake out of your head your stupid Mind of judgement! '

Why do you think Jesus freaked out in the market of the money lenders and shareholders? They were the liars which Mind control you in Judgement and call you in to be unknowingly imprisoned and to sell yourself for a cheap fee just to get through the next day, shackling people in their need to survive and taking their freedom away in indebtedness to the energies of fear born from greed. Even Jesus couldn't reason with them. He had to turn those tables over and probably give a few of them a sharp shock to stop their murderous cruel ways in the sacred temple.

How much relationship emotional currency that we get indebted to which also robs us of our freedom in a false sense of the bank of morality. From childhood we have emotional debt we feel the burning need to pay to the people who say they love us because they saved us from the fear of being alone. Fear is a debt that no one can ever pay off.

So put your hands up and go bankrupt to Spirit then you will realise you were always the wealthiest man on the planet anyway.

# CHAPTER 15

# HARMONY OF
# SPIRIT & SOUL

I am keen that you understand that although I have lived an extraordinary life to some extent I have not lived one free of pain and sadness. I have experienced great highs and lows as everybody else does. I am no different to you.

At one particular low point in my life when I felt great sorrow I sought inspiration from God. I want to share with you something I wrote at one of my darkest times and the answer that came.

THE PRAYER

'God who am I if not a Spirit formed out of creation? I feel at times so alone with the sadness and fears which life has dealt me. Is it really my own choosing? Lost on the edge of living life and feeling safe in imaginary hopes and dreams.

Who am I? Do I give in to the struggle, give in to the lies and the hypocrites?

Great Mother, Father help me wash these stains of sadness from my Soul.

Who am I? Take me home.'

GOD'S ANSWER

'You are a son of God. Your Spirit is Divine. As part of creation you are a living consciousness.

You are a freed Spirit dropped into the pool of life, moulded by the physical rules of nature with all the fears that manifest from detachment. Yet you are not truly detached. You are living in Gods' life.

You are part of creation forming new perfection. I am you. You are the beginning and the end. Look around you. Everywhere you look everything talks to you and carries the same pure essence of flow.

Imagine, in the beginning there is only one giant Spirit. As life's consciousness starts to flow out into eternity you know moments of pure perfection with one new ingredient, the will to experience for itself through thought and the law of manifestation and rejection, like a cell divides into two, potential to manifest into whatever form life will hold it, being free to flower into things not yet thought that it could be. This is why consciousness has evolved to create this perfect vehicle of its Divine expression, the grace of will came and divided it into sparks of consciousness.

Individuality experiencing duality.

The end result of the journey of the Spirit is, imagine when the matter universe has expanded until its end when even matter ceases to exist leaving only emotional consciousness forming a new universe made from awareness of itself, a completed expression of a fluid source of manifestation, the next step in the evolution of Spirit. Instead of a material universe a total emotional universe spiritually free to manifest creation.'

This came to me sitting in a car park on a grey miserable day, feeling empty and alone, in May 1995.

I have considered this along with the many other Spiritual revelations I have had and can truthfully say I believe we are all connected to everything all of the time. I believe each atom has a consciousness in its own way.

It is because we can't deal with the Omnipresence of this vast universe that we have had to bring it down into human form, into shapes we can relate to, lesser Gods, smaller bite size pieces to make it all more acceptable and comprehendible forming archetypal personalities.

## SENTIENT BEINGS

The link that bridges both worlds, the human and the Spirit, is the energy we share as sentient beings. Here on Earth we know and recognise that energy as being the pure honest feelings of our Spirit without Mind's duality. The byproduct of our feelings is turned into emotion and held in Mind's memory.

Thoughts have their own energy but when turned into an emotion by the conceptual Mind then the energy is amplified into short term suffering of Mind's desires. Feelings, not emotions, are very powerful in helping us create things. If we are driven by this pure feeling of Spirit we can create with excited anticipation and manifest yet unthought-of marvels into the universe. I am talking of feeling and emotion as two separate experiences. Emotion is of the Mind but pure feeling is eternity manifesting creation.

Emotions link with everything. When negative things happen we sometimes hold in those emotions with often crippling results in one way or another. But in the same way emotion, when we get thrilled about something, is a beautiful energy and moves us forward to reach out for our dreams.

They are a tool we use to either empower us or disempower us but because they are emotions created from Mind they are both the same penny.

You think your emotion is your identity of who you are but you are not your emotion. That belongs to the rulership of the Mind. You are Spirit allowing emotion to form personality and all personality sooner or later dies but the magnificence of your Spirit that this lives through is always here in the absolute expression of Love.

Every day we see many negative emotions on the television and in the newspapers and it can easily swamp our day. Once again it is no use us trying to dissociate from this world we live in but neither do we need to overly dwell in the sadness, stresses and strains of it all. Try not to automatically reach for the TV remote control. Learn to sit and just be for ten to twenty minutes a day rather than twenty minutes of violence, bad language, impossible situations, arguments and strife. Allow yourself to become important and in that time your brain can relax and then expand. Allow yourself to hear your own inspiration.

## LIVING IN A BOXED IN WORLD

Isn't it funny how we sit on box shaped furniture in box shaped rooms and watch box shaped televisions? We eat on box shaped tables, we drive boxed shaped cars looking through box shaped windows, go to work in a box shaped room and box in our feelings and thoughts. Then we die in a box shaped coffin. Yet there is nothing box shaped about us in body and Spirit. There are no square bits in the physical body and there is nothing square about the wind, the rain, the trees, the flowers, the animals, the sun, the moon and the stars. There is nothing square about us as sentient beings.

So leave the box behind for just an afternoon, a weekend, get outside, do something you love, see how much lighter you feel. You can consciously lift yourself up and raise your Spirit.

## LOSING CONNECTION TO THE EARTH

In the last hundred years we have made more and more man made luxuries, more and more demands, but we have lost our connection to the Earth, to nature, to the true cycle, to Spirituality. We took our need for survival to extremes, way past survival, to the point where we are at war with one another, constantly looking for more and becoming masters of destruction. We will soon get to the point where there is no humanness left anymore and no individuality. When man evolved materialistically we could grow crops, we drove cars, we looked at different philosophies and all of these things became part of us. There were those that had and those that didn't and we needed some kind of justification so we made up all kinds of rules and regimes and beliefs. Structures were brought in to control society. Those at the top did not want us to recognise our own individual power or our own ability so they made our natural connection to the Earth a bad thing in league with the Devil himself. This went hand in hand with the belief that you should then only contact God via a priest or some other third party. So in our need to survive we destroyed our faith in the wonder of our own human Spirit.

We only dance in this world for a short while. Let's not disempower the beauty within. We have forgotten how beautiful we are and we have layered it with survival and fear but the greatest power is freedom. The balance we seek is to balance our Soul journey with our Spiritual journey and the need to evolve, to flow and to create.

## FLOWING

A great deal of unhappiness stems from the inability to allow our lives and relationships to flow. We find something we like and try to always keep it the same, fixed within rigid boundaries. This doesn't often keep things the same but can stifle people and situations so much that change comes about anyway. Better to make change from choice rather than change that circumstance dictates.

We are beginning to uncover our core once more, bringing our emotions into a chrysalis, pushing us back into the awareness of who we really are.

It is about getting people to take responsibility for their own lives and the way they live, to inspire people to dance in this world by being human. We need our relationships if they are valid and inspire us. To be frail, afraid and uncertain are all part of being human. Let's be spiritually alive, not by looking for a crutch to depend on but by embracing who we are and rejoicing in our humanness. We do not need to fight with life. We do not need to fight to survive but we do need to realise our Spirit is eternal and then we can relax and enjoy life. We don't have to abandon our luxuries to work in tune with nature we simply need to use our intellect to devise new practices that are healthy for us and the environment in which we live.

# CHAPTER 16

# MANIFESTATION

The universe we live in operates under certain laws. A very important one that we have yet to come to grips with properly is The Law of Manifestation. You have probably heard of the Law of Attraction which in real terms can be translated as The Law of Your Will to Manifest or should I say using the emotional Mind's belief to attract, but actually it does not work. There are many books and great thinkers who have said, 'You can change your life and have all that you want if you change the way you think.' These are usually based on wanting happy, healthy relationships and material wealth and only if you know the secret of using your thoughts correctly and sending them out will they then manifest into your life.

They have formulated hundreds of ways to do this process but the main one is emotional visualization through imagery to get your Mind reprogrammed into a positive desire and then releasing those thoughts to create manifestation of your energetic emotional will.

The other form of programming is breaking your negative habituated thought patterns with new positive habituated thought patterns. The truth is it does not fully work and falls short in creating true love, joy and happiness. I know because I have tried it and so have many of my friends. I have tried emotionally feeling good about the things I desire and want, visualizing how my life would be when I had everything and how good I would feel. Even visually having photos and music played daily to get my intentions focused on my dream that for sure would happen, if not now then maybe ten years down the line. It is just another Mind's lie that gives you the feel good factor without the reality.

The Law of Attraction in Mind's desire is another twisted lie that imprisons you even more in suffering.

It is an ugly money making exercise through the many 'false prophets' selling conceptualized Spiritual wisdom in motivational empowerment.

There is a way to honestly, truly manifest what you truly want. I will show you later in this chapter.

It is your Spirit's desire that actually manifests what you truly want. That is the only true way to manifest what you want not through the desires of the Mind. Desires of the Mind tell you that whatever you think you want is only achieved when absolutely focused on creating it. In reality it cannot be manifested out of your Mind's habituated patterns that forms your Mind's Soul personality and which in itself is not who you are. So how can who you are not create what you think you desire? Even if you want to create a new false positive personality, which is not who you are either, how could it ever create an honest congruent reality? That is why it doesn't work. The Law of Attraction really says, 'If you focus on your dreams absolutely powered with Mind's emotion then it will be given to you.' It simply does not work because it is born on false ego's desire.

The truth is that whatever you think you want and whatever your ego desires you don't get but whatever you are you attract. Only like attracts like. You are constantly manifesting in the unknown person of who you think you are. You can tell who you are by what you attract. What you attract is born from your deeply embedded fear based hidden beliefs, not what you want.

Bizarrely though that too isn't who you are. So we are all pretty stuffed!

That is why you hear people say, 'Why do I always attract this rubbish and horrible life because I certainly don't call for it?'

Of course you don't call for it but you have already created a persona that is so complicated in fear based identity you can't even see the habituated patterns that manifest your reality.

I am not one of those people who are into, 'Change the way you think and your life will change.' Yes you can change the way you think but usually into a false personality and a kind of hoping if you fake it you will make it. It doesn't work. Yes you do change but only into another story shaped by your emotional Mind's will.

There are many Spiritual innovators selling you Spiritual secrets and knowledge that will redeem you and save you but they are the ones that use this as cruel Spiritual exploitation. The only way to change is to stop living in your Mind. Stop reinforcing Mind's belief.

The moment you stop you will light up without any effort and will start to attract your Spirit's desire which is freedom, love and joy. That is your natural state.

I know you just don't believe that honestly but you totally believe though that you must find it somewhere out there in a place or a person or in Mind's dream searched for by a Mind that doesn't really know what it is looking for! How fascinating?

This is the universe saying, 'Yes you can have whatever you want and whatever you think about with conviction and repetition.'

The trouble is most of the human population are not aware that they are manifesting at all. We manifest by thinking about something several times, giving emotions to fleeting thoughts on empty desires.

Well guess what? Our world is filled with negative images and thoughts and these vibrate at a low frequency and we therefore attract low vibration situations and people into our lives. We may do this consciously or subconsciously because we don't really stop to consider most of the thousands of thoughts a day that we have. We may think about something we want like a new relationship or more money in one thought and it may even feel good when we imagine it. However, all too often our very next thought goes along the lines of, 'Nothing good ever happens to me. I'm not that clever so I will never earn that much money. I don't look good enough,' and so it goes on.

Again a lot of this comes down to our programming and past learning. Old habits die hard so we sabotage our own good.

The universe does not discern what is good or bad for us it merely answers our thoughts. If we have been programmed to a lower vibration or if we have low self-worth and we believe that all we can expect from life is struggle and hardship, then the universe simply mirrors those wishes and sends us more and more of it.

We are all mirrors of Mind's desire.

Now let's give you the traditional positive talk!

'We need high frequency thoughts because if we feel good, happy, excited and ambitious about life and have fire in our hearts then that too is what we can expect to receive.

When we realise how this works we can start to control our thoughts and positively invite into our life the things we truly would love to have or experience.

If your programming has been negative up to this point, it is not too late. You simply have to decide enough is enough and do something to pull yourself back up to the higher vibratory thought patterns. This is really wonderful, positive and good for you. Let's change our lives today, this second! Let's jump with joy with this new positive programming! '

Guess what? That doesn't work either because they are both one and the same desires! I have done all that stuff to the point where I just feel like throwing up and puking over the garden fence in this pious nonsense! All short term plasters over weeping wounds that you get ultimately through desire's Mind. What I begin to see here is that yes, being positive and lifting yourself up and getting on with things feels good but it is always in the shadow of, 'What if it goes wrong?'

In fact you haven't moved one inch spiritually. Mankind is still in the habituated cycle of survival at any cost and at any pretended emotional good. If we are going to punch through into what we really are and what this is all about then we cannot be defined in Mind's dream. This is leading to the whole of humanity needing to look within itself and becoming deeply aware. If all of us are aware individually of who we are then we can free ourselves from the awful restriction of our Minds into the magnificence and perfection that we are in responsibility of the grace and love as one world and one people.

We have to stop whoring out our Spirit to the mind.

All thoughts are energy and when projected manifest cause and effect. How far it reaches depends on who is manifesting, your Mind or your spirit?

The low level acquiring Mind only ever manifests energetically short term feel good factors and is hard work. The energetic energy of your Spirit manifests long term awakened love and freedom which is the living power of who you are forever without any effort.

Which one do you choose? The lie or the Truth?

This is why it is truly beneficial for your Soul and Spirit to be in harmony. Your Spirit only wants what is best for you but your Soul gets confused by the layers of disbelief it is cloaked in. This is why we often swing through peaks and troughs, highs and lows, ultimately not really achieving our dreams or moving forward to any great extent.

PERFECT DAY THOUGHT

So how do we truly manifest?

Well the first question is whether what I want to manifest is grown from my Mind or my heart centered in Spirit?

Is it the calling of Spirit or the calling of Mind's desire?

We also need to know how we ask the Universal Consciousness to manifest what we desire. We have a contract with the God within us (Spirit) and the contract says this, 'Whatever you ask for I will give you without question.' When your Spirit calls of itself, which is strangely unwanting without desire it has only needs of expression in being and feeling, God pours out what you need, even more than you need. (How mad is that? It doesn't make sense.)

When asked from Mind there is always a duality. This is not the same as three wishes because God is saying, 'You can have as many wishes as you want forever and my contract is that I will give them to you and that is the deal,' and that is the truth.

To understand this, when we ask the God within us or desire something we really, really want we send those thoughts out to the Universe and God says, 'I am going to go and get your wishes.'

And as God is about to vanish and start manifesting your will, your Mind says, 'I don't want a house that big. I don't want a relationship that I know will go wrong. I only need that much money because I don't deserve any more than I have just asked for.'

And God says, 'I will go and get that too because I never say no to anything you want.'

God sends you whatever you emotionally dwell upon so if you spend the majority of your time living in scarcity and disempowerment God doesn't say, 'I am going to fix it for you,' God says, 'Well that is the energy you like so I will give you loads more but I don't know what you are going to do with it!'

And when you are feeling really good and life is going well and you feel emotionally good then God says, 'I will give you loads more of that too. I don't know what you will do with it though but that's what you want!'

He doesn't say that feeling good is the right way to go. In this manifestation of emotional will God does not care whether it is good or bad because the contract is, 'Whatever you desire you will be given even if you decide to create new worlds.'

The only sacred contract with God is whatever you ask for I will give you. This is the only sacred contract we have ever made before humanity took its first breath.

But can you see that both these desires of acquirement are from Mind not from Spirit which in itself is a powerful force. Your desire to manifest needs to come from somewhere else. It needs to come from the silence and peace within you. From your awakened Spirit which can only dream creation into existence through loving thoughts, not love of thoughts but through loving thoughts. The Truth is, if you ask your Spirit it absolutely does not want anything! But your Mind will say, 'Don't be crazy. You have got to want something.'

And your Spirit will answer, 'No I don't want anything,' and when you absolutely know that you become everything that you desire because in your Spirit's not wanting is the true desire of uncontrolled manifestation.

Spirit desire does not manifest from emotional will. Spirit's desire is life's longing revealing itself with gentleness and love which is what you are and the God within says, 'You don't have to ask me like your Mind does, I naturally always manifest your free will in love in perfect day wanting in heart's dreams which is the dance of your living life force in the present moment.'

Let's look at it another way. You may not have noticed but there is a difference when you have a non-wanting thought that is not premeditated from fear based desire.

These are thoughts like, 'I enjoyed that' or I used to enjoy going to the cinema or the theatre or out for a meal,' then you have a little daydream and just say to yourself, 'I really liked that,' and it just feels good. It feels warm.

Then your Mind kicks in and says, 'I am too busy. I can't do that. I can't afford that. I need somebody to share that with,' and so you just let it go.

But that simple daydream wasn't wanting. It was just feeling good about something you liked. And isn't it funny how within a couple of days of having that simple little thought someone comes to you and says, 'Hey look I have two free tickets to the cinema and you can have them,' or someone says, 'Hey I will take you out for a meal or to the theatre,' out of the blue.

These are the thoughts that truly manifest your desire. And why is it that all the things you positively, forcibly absolutely want and desire you never seem to get? It is because they are born from fear and Mind's will to be the master of your life being who you think you are.

The way to manifest what you want is called a 'Perfect Day Thought'. The perfect day thought is your lovely daydream within your heart and the moment you have that thought it begins to manifest because it is not a desiring thought, it is a 'being' thought, it is not a thought with boundaries and these are not fantasy dreams. It doesn't matter about not having the money, the right job, the power or the contacts because you do not have to work out the bit in between. It is a thought not born from ego's desire. The perfect day thought is imagining in gentleness and joy just for fun.

If you could close your eyes without any restraint or fear in lovely daydream and imagine where you would like to live and it doesn't matter whether it is a tent or a mansion or a log cabin. What would your house look like that you would feel at peace in?

Not a place where if you have got the money and the power you could buy anything you want and where you would be too busy looking good and making a great showroom for the world. That is ego's desire. If it was exactly as it pleases your Spirit and no one else what would your house look like? What would your living room look like? What would every room in the house look like and feel like? Even how would you have your cup of tea in the morning or place your slippers by the side of the bed. If you had a cat or a dog what would they look like? Who would be in your house with you? How they would be feeling happy and content, as you would be, because this is not a home of the Mind but a beautiful loving home where you sit within your Spirit content and at peace.

Then you just let that thought go and guess what? The universe starts doing its work. Without you even trying or desiring it just begins to manifest and it works 100% of the time. You will see fortuitous circumstances unfold and present themselves out of the blue.

One day in a reading at a woman's house she asked me, 'How can I truly have everything I want?'

So I told her about the perfect day thought. Then I went on to tell her a story about a man who I told to have the perfect day thought to manifest what he would truly like.

And he said to me, 'I can imagine what would make me feel really happy and peaceful just for myself. A house in the countryside with beautiful gardens and a path leading up to the front door. The house would have open fires, wooden floors, and be in an old style away from the madding crowd in a peaceful place. It would have a garden with apple trees, pear trees and the most beautiful panoramic views over the sea and be a place where I could find peace. '

He just imagined how every part of it would look and feel, and by the way, at the time, this man had not a hope in hell of ever affording anything such as that and was actually spending a lot of his time living in a tent at weekends but within three months he was living in that place.

And the woman said, 'Wow that is amazing!'

And I said, 'That is a true story and by the way, that man was me.' I even showed her some pictures on my mobile phone of this beautiful place and my gardens.

The secret is not that you will have it only when you have got all the controlling things in place to get what you want, it is dreaming in your life in an understanding of how the perfect day thought works. There is no ego or Mind's desire only love and joy of heart's desire. It works always but at the same time it is always sabotaged and disempowered by Mind's loveless dreams. The only burning desire that works is the fire of your Spirit untethered from your Mind. These desires are naturally released from your Spirit that shares its love in all that it manifests. Isn't it strange how even if you look around where you live and the things you have, some of the things you see were born and given to you from your perfect day thoughts like spiritual icons reminding you that all the other possessions, which you are not comfortable with, were created from Mind's fear based desire like an eclectic montage of truth and lies.

## THE LIES OF WORRYING

You are already more aware of yourself just by reading this far and you will have inevitably thought about yourself. So the next time you are aware of being dragged down to a lower frequency thought grab yourself. Stop feeding it in your head, stop feeding it emotionally, stop all the, 'They said this and they did that,' or, 'I'm worried about this,' and look at how it all piles on top of you.

What is it doing for you? It makes you want to run away and it makes you feel negative and low. Although in a way this is also good for you as you get to a point where you either give up or decide to fight. The intellect kicks in and says 'No way am I having that' or 'I can't because I am not that strong. I need help.' You either need somebody to motivate you or you stand back to evaluate what is really going on.

Give yourself a breather. Nil by head! Don't do anything and just be still.

Try not to think about those worries for a short while so your body can power up again and take time out. Then when you look again you will see a way to deal with whatever has cropped up. When your Mind is not dressed in the emotional situations then your path starts coming back and when it comes back you either find the answers to it or you release it. Negative emotions can make you feel embittered, lost, disempowered and ill so try to concentrate on those things in your life that you are grateful for and count your blessings, no matter how small. Maybe it is your children, your view, your partner, your friend or your pet. If you like to meditate retreat for a while to your safe space, your tranquil place. One of my safe spaces is to imagine myself looking at the stars or as a child being by the sea. Allow yourself to come back to balance within yourself, don't add to the mountain of worry.

You cannot worry yourself sick to be well. You cannot worry for another so that they won't suffer. You cannot worry for the future that does not exist. Worrying is not martyring yourself to God so God will give you favour. It is all another Mind's lie. Worry is born from past fears and dwells in future fears which do not exist. To end worry you must change the word itself in your Mind to the word 'concern' that lives in the present moment in honest reality. Concern will say 'Your children right now are all well and safe or they need help right now' in truth. Usually all is well, only fearful worrying turns you into a martyr of the Mind.

## LOOKING FOR PEACE

I am waiting for an external God's voice to show me the way. Any thoughts that you have that give you a sense of lack, suffering or fear are your Mind living your life. You can become very aware of this when you just stop and be still at peace with yourself. At peace, not in peace with yourself. You stop engaging thoughts. Instead just become being, just here, in the silent awareness with no thoughts, not even thinking that you have to do this. In your stillness and peace is who you are. In the moment you sit with yourself at peace then you see the world as a different place. Worries and problems don't attack you to create an energetic or aggressive reaction because your peace already has the answer and it is not wanting of anything of Mind's desire.

Have you noticed that when you look at your problems your Mind jumps in there with worry and judgement and the whole process feels uncomfortable? It actually feels wrong but in its bizarre way it fires you up to react to the situation to fight for survival but even in that is suffering. It is like a big bubble of that suffering thought and it is all uncomfortable because it is not even true. Your silent witness within does not know anger or suffering it is just who you are. The Mind confuses survival with a strange Mind's desire which in itself is fear but when at peace with yourself the world is brighter. You feel safe within yourself and you can cope without trying.

You just bring your peace into you every moment you can and sit within your peace, not peaceful but the peace of surrender that releases the aggressive

Mind's dream. That is where your freedom and love lies always.

Any form of suffering you experience is the Mind in control of you until you just stop in peace. You don't have to become a guru or have moments of Onenesss or have a Spiritual shield, which in itself is elitist crud, because you are the peace that you desire. Just be it. Know it. Feel it. Don't look for it. Don't think you hold it for a moment and then it is gone because that is just another Mind bubble, another story.

You are God's peace by nature. It is only in the peace of your Spirit that you can see the truth of the world. Your peace only sees two things, absolute reality and exactly what is the truth in the very present moment. Being in peace is being perfectly still, silent, not quiet. When you can sit perfectly still in peace and silence then you will see the world through the eyes of God. Your body will be filled with centered natural energy and you will feel truly alive. And all Mind's thoughts are turned into an asteroid belt that slowly spins around you, emotionally unattached, no longer draining your life force and only to be observed as curiosities.

## FOOD OF EGO

It's time to put the kettle on and get something to eat but even doing that in your peace is a pleasure not a chore. What I am trying to say is you either live with the suffering Mind or you choose not to. It is that simple.

You have to choose to be at peace even though your habituated life and Mind, born out of Mind's suffering, is forever calling you to join humanities' lie. You can make a cup of tea just because you are here in peace and it is enjoyable. If you make a cup of tea out of habituated necessity it becomes a suffering cup of tea. Same teapot in reality but a different teapot in Mind's dream.

You can cook a meal for your family while they sit in the other room playing and being happy in their space. You can enjoy cooking it out of love in your heart because you just are and it is peaceful. It is not wanting, it is just doing and everyone gets fed more than just the food because it is food cooked with love.

Then there is the dinner of the Mind where everything has to be just perfect, the right temperature, all as expected, as the world thinks it should be done and those who eat it are supposed to appreciate it because it is cooked so perfectly. All that expectation and that food only fills your stomach and feels empty, loveless and pretended even though in judgement's Mind it is thought to be better than a meal cooked from the heart of just being at peace.

Food or anything shared with love, not thinking of love or finding love, but in your joyous Spirit's peaceful Love, is always remembered in the hearts of those who are fed or kindness shared.

Food of ego is suffering in every bite. How do you reckon murder burgers stand up to that? Is there Love in it or is there suffering in every bite from the hands of greed?

I would rather be hungry and eat a dry loaf of bread with a good friend than have the best 10 course meal with people who do not care.

# CHAPTER 17

# CHOICES

Making choices is the most difficult thing we do in our life. Not the simple choices but choices that resonate around us and affect us. It is not the choices of the small stuff but making the choices to be happy. There are two kinds of choices.

There are the choices we make every day with problems which we all do. The first choice is the short term choices such as, 'What shall I eat? What shall I wear today? Should I even bother to get up or just stay in bed? Whose side should I take in the argument?' or, 'What thing can I do to please the expectations of others?' They are all short term but have you noticed the moment we shift from simple choices of what we eat and how we dress to doing what people expect of us then the expectation choices all feel like putting plasters over weeping wounds. It is like playing for time just to be accepted. And when you have got a hundred of those choices pressing upon you then you fall into some kind of shell shock and give your choices and power to others to control your life and make decisions for you because you are weak, not knowing which way to really turn, still only making more short term choices that just keep things at bay.

Then we have the big choices. There are those choices that change your journey, whether it is running away or being positively empowered to manifest. Both are actually scary and uncertain, it is just that they have more emotional value.

So let's go away from the big choices and go back to the little ones that make us feel shell shocked with our heads spinning but we can cope with them and maybe when they are all sorted we will find the answers to the big ones. This is like a no win situation which is exactly what it is. Both of them disempower you. In a world where you are forced and told to always make the right choices which are the right ones?

So here we go again, back into some kind of shell shock that drains us and makes us feel tired and weak. While in that position all the demons of negative self-worth jump on your back and pull you back into addictive behavior patterns just to get you through the next day.

But can't you see that the choice process is built on your addictive behavior patterns and your codependencies which are all fear based? You can't win and it drives you mad leaving you feeling numb and powerless.

The funny thing is, from the moment we open our eyes, our life is making choices all held in the hands of judgement.

Over the years we end up not bothering to even make any big choices. They are just too hard so we keep our choices simple. We do anything to be accepted and not to be questioned or rock the boat and so we become grey people. We think, 'Hey. That is better than being rejected,' but then this leaves us totally open to be abused by greed, tradition and religion.

I know this all sounds dark and grim but this is your best friend, the monkey on your back. The monkey on your back grows with you and gets bigger and bigger until it turns into a gorilla which is hard to carry around. The gorilla is your excuses all lined up so you don't have to make any more choices because they all seem to lead to suffering turning you into a coward in daring to choose for yourself. So I guess we are pretty stuffed! What do we do?

The truth is the way you feel right now you either have lots of choices, which are all uncertain anyway, or if you are bottom line, you have two choices.

## TWO CHOICES – LIVE OR DIE

There are never less than two choices.

The two ultimate choices are live or die. We know that but for some reason we often don't have the power within us to make a conscious decision. A real conscious decision is like stepping out the plane with your parachute on. You are not coming back but your parachute definitely opens. When you land do you hit the ground with a thud or do you hit it running?

Conscious decisions are those which powerfully free us and then once it is done the doorway is flung open for new journeys. It is in God's hands.

When we are younger these are easy to make for we have long lives and are unaware of the consequences. As we get older and more responsible we fear the big decisions but something in us keeps pushing us to make them but then we resist them in liberal mediocre justification. So we end up only making the big decisions when we are really forced to or they are made for us by others.

Both are life sapping and drudgery. So we just stand in shell shock.

## HOW DO WE BREAK THE SHACKLE?

So how do we break the shackle? It is just being alive and doing anything because if we just sit in our judgement Mind it loves you being there. It has its own cruel clever way of robbing you of your personal freedom and power to even question yourself. Your Mind will even pretend to offer you the freedom to change your life, to be more positive but that too is its lie because what chases both of those is Mind's fear. So we look outside of ourselves for someone or something to give us the will to be free and live again with purpose but we can never find it because everyone is living in the same place. The ones that appear to be free are successful and fake sincerity well.

The only way is to surrender to all those thoughts and all those choices because not one of them ultimately is true. We seem to think if we abandon choice then life has no purpose and we are nothing. The day you abandon choice is the day you abandon Mind's desire that creates the choices of your imprisonment.

## CONSCIOUS CHOICE OF DIVINE WILL

If you just stop and let go for a moment and be still, at peace, without choices, you can feel an energy of consciousness rising up from within you which in its not wanting offers you universal infinite possibilities not built on desire. This conscious choice is divine will which is in your Spirit flowing within you and out from you only leading you to decisions where you are free and safe. That is the choice of Spirit. There is no suffering in it and it is very gentle but has the strength of the universe. Your Spirit only ever has one choice - Love.

The only choice you ever need to make is to trust absolutely the love of the peace and the stillness within yourself and from that all the doorways in your life lead you to making honest conscious decisions that enhance your life with real purpose. You don't even have to work it out. Just try it for an hour. Try it for a day and you will see just by doing that providence will present itself to you.

As life unfolds in this new faith of Spirit you will acquire your unwavering security within you through your inner Spiritual voice of honesty and freedom. This is your true nature. As I say this I know you just don't believe it because you are still judging this from Mind's judgement and conceptuality which is only how your Mind makes choices. When you are free of your Mind it is no longer the decision maker, or the controller of your life, or your platform of who you think you are. You suddenly find there is another you which is full of life and doesn't need your Mind's permission for anything. Your Mind is not who you are. It is just a tool to make logical decisions not emotional decisions.

Even if you resist what I am saying the resistance is the bubble of your Mind again just telling you that it knows better. Your Mind will tell you that it will find the answers in its choices all formed from fear. The voice in you that knows that you need to let go of your Mind's grip is also the Mind's grip around your throat. You can let that go too for it is not even real. Even if you think for a second, 'I don't understand and I can't,' that again is the Mind. Just know that is not who you are. You are this peace and silence here within you always.

I dare you to let go of your Mind's choices without question or judgement and suddenly you will find the same world looks like a better place because in reality the real world is beautiful. Just know that the Mind is the demon of judgement and choices are also one of its biggest allies. You have to stop your Mind's corrupted choices from taking your beautiful vibrant flowing life's energy and turning it into feeling that life is futile if your Mind is not in control. For even those thoughts are again your Mind robbing you.

You can't beat the Mind with another thought or another strategy or a clever meditation or clever words from the prophets. They are all just tasters of freedom.

## AMBASSADOR OF SPIRIT

You become your own prophet and ambassador of your Spirit by no longer letting your Mind run your life with all its imprisoning false and malicious drama. You don't need any of this for you are already free right now and the voice that does not believe it is your Mind. The voice that knows this is true is your Spirit.

As I say this you may feel a fear conjured from your Mind in its questioning again wrapped in some bizarre emotional feeling. This again is your damn Mind! It only has a hold on you because you trust it with your very life but it will take your life and run your life until you are dead in all of its struggle and suffering.

On your last breath you say to your Mind, 'Why did I suffer? I am scared,'

And your Mind will say to you, 'That is what I do stupid!'

The Mind appears to be living and clever like it is you but really it is not living. It only takes your feelings and turns them into emotions which makes you think that it has intelligence of its own and this tells you, 'This is who you are' The Mind fakes knowing you with emotion. Your Mind is not an independent thinker or a being. It is just your Mind. The Mind identifies itself by taking your feelings and painting an emotional story so you believe your Mind to be real and alive and who you are. That is what we do every second of every day but really it is a fake which pretends reality and the moment you stop thinking, the authentic you presents itself in its vastness and beauty and intelligence beyond belief. Your Mind is a bit like this old story.

## TURTLES AND SCORPIONS

This is a story from the Native American Indians. There were once two islands and on these islands lived turtles and scorpions. On one particular island the scorpion (which is your Mind) said to the turtle,

'You know we have not always got on and we kill you but turtle, we know there is a big storm coming and this island will sink under the waves and we will all surely die. We don't swim but we have decided to make a pact with you. We will never sting you again or kill you and we will become friends and live in harmony if you carry us to the other island on your backs where we will all be safe.'

The turtle said, 'We have learnt not to trust you.'

And the scorpion answered him, 'This is life and death. We need to live and if you save us we will never harm you again. I absolutely promise for I am King of the scorpions.'

So the turtle, and all the other turtles, agreed to carry the scorpions on their backs to safety.

The storm came and thousands of turtles were swimming across the sea to the island each one with a scorpion on its back (or maybe I should say monkey? No, I will stay with scorpions) and then, when they were half way across, the scorpion stung the turtle.

The turtle said, 'Why have you done that? We will both die now.'

And the scorpion said, 'I am a scorpion. That is what I do.'

Do you see your Mind is the scorpion and that is what it does? It kills you. It doesn't understand what death is but pretends to care about it.

We have to understand that our Mind is not who we are and any suffering we ever have and any fear is born from Mind's embrace that cruelly survives us and in the same process slowly kills us.

We don't have to wait until we die to be free. We have to let our Mind die to the belief that it is our

master, while we are living so we can be free. That is
the Mind of our suffering, which some people call
the ego Mind, but it is bigger than that. Our Mind is a
tool that helps us create the things we wish to
experience. That is its job. We have to let our Mind
become its ego but become egoless then it does its
job to help us live our lives congruently.

## THE SHIP OF THE MIND

We just have to jump the ship of the Mind, or should
I say the luxury cruise ship of our Mind. Do it now
without thinking and without knowing why. Just let
its tethering free. Let the ship float away and leave
you on the shores of your Spirit in a land full of
colour, love, fruit and promise. This is the Shangri la
you came from. Don't become your Mind's slave
because that is all you are. A slave to a Mind that
doesn't care but only pretends to. Stop being a slave.
Mind slaves are what the majority of us are all slowly
creating prisons in the physical to die in. That is all
the Mind can ever truly offer you.

Believe me people in real jails are far more free, freer
than those who live in Mind's imprisonment. The
thing though with the prison of the Mind is there are
no doors. You are free to walk out into the light at
any time. It is the light of who you are and you are
the light always. It is hard to ask you to follow or

become who you are when there is no bench mark or foundation to work from in a physical form.

I could say the foundation is the Love that you are but just by using those words it throws the whole concept out the window because your Mind will just grab that concept and say, 'What the hell is Love?' and then the same Mind will tell you, 'I will tell you what love is.'

You see what I am trying to say is your Mind claims every thought only because you absolutely believe your Mind to be true. You believe that your Mind is your best friend. The truth is it is not true. This is not who you are and the only way you will know it is to surrender to Spirit and be at peace.

With both the words 'surrender 'and 'peace' what I mean is just 'surrender' not, 'What is surrendering?' and, 'Be at peace,' not knowing what peace is. That is where your Spirit dwells which is in you right now, alive, full of love, joy and freedom.

But as I say this to you I am trying to talk to your Spirit through your ugly Mind of judgement and reasoning. Just accept that you are God in disguise, not God as a concept or, 'What is God?' Just hold the word God and that is who you are. God is the invisible that is visible in everything that is seen and experienced, which is you too.

Do you understand what I am saying?

Don't you dare for a second intellectualise this! You are awake and have never been asleep.

## GOODNESS WITHIN

Have you noticed the more you suffer there is a yearning or a longing within that knows what is good. It is the goodness within you not the goodness of acquirement. It knows this force or energy that is in you and around you always and the Mind subconsciously fears to identify with it, that invisible force, that silent witness that speaks a thousand words and unseen sees all things. That emotion that feels all things without one moment of thought presents itself to you constantly but, strangely, it is hard for you to turn your face and look within and recognize as your absolute true self this magnificence of Spirit which longs to become the Love that you are, expressing itself in all that you are, this very moment and without one bar or one chain of emotion or control of Mind's cancer.

We are showing that we are all diamonds being chipped away by life's calling to know ourselves until at some point our facets become our shining lights and examples to all around as ambassadors, all of us, to our Holy Spirit within and the awakened Love that we are.

I AM SPIRIT.

Spirit is not something that can be looked at through the eyes, measured or shaped, talked about or compared or held. That is not your Spirit.

Your Spirit is the life force alive right now within you that cannot be touched or seen or described. When you try to find it you get confused.

Only the still and silent Mind in the present moment senses your Spirit. Only then can the sacred arise and reveal itself in who you are.

You can perceive the whole world from it. You can perceive the 'One' from it and feel that you are 'One' but you can't look at it with looking.

You can't think about what exists before thought. Your Spirit is the eternal witness of your Soul's journey. It does not exist in time. You can't grab the timeless with anything in time.

Your ego Mind desperately fears and won't allow you to let go or relax its hold over you and always pulls you back to look into the past and the future and to fear mortality. Your Spirit is here and now this very second.

It is this sense of life that you are aware of' that gives you life this very moment. It asks nothing of you but it is you.

The Spirit within reveals itself when you are honestly honest. Once you surrender your Mind it instantly reveals itself in who you are.

You are always fully present and fully awakened. This is your natural state.

Your Spirit was never born and never dies. It has always been here as part of Oneness. It is only our Mind that has taken us so far away out of our natural state, so far out of alignment with the Truth and the natural world.

Your Mind always takes you out of the present moment. Its identity and existence is only formed when it is out of the present moment creating the world of dream, drama and illusion.

All natural living things upon the planet are simply here in complete and absolute reality. We are the only species upon this planet that can make itself believe that it is not part of it in Mind's dream.

Your Mind habitually takes you into the world of not being your full awakened self.

The only way you can leave the present moment is to think yourself out of it and by thinking we compare from the past and plan the future but the Mind can only shape into prisons of your Spirit.

Thinking by itself is magnificent but when thinking becomes your identity it creates death and misery and imprisonment all around it, even to your physical form.

The bars of the Mind, each bar is called suffering. Your beautiful magnificent Spirit is the nothing at all within you but when released with a loving open heart it fills everything within you and around you with the absolute Love and Joy that you are forever.

The nothing that you are within is the most alive vibrant shining noisy voice of the Oneness that you are. It is who you are but when observed, the 'Who' vanishes and turns into 'I AM' alive. Aliveness forever living as the feeling and the voice of God that your whole world and form has been born through.

We are the awakened of what has always been awake for eternity. It can never be suffering or less.

The moment you let go of Mind and desire in the awakened stillness the Holy witness of who you are becomes the witness to all other Spirits upon this Earth. They all turn and look and see your Holy Spirit and become aware at the same time of their Holy Spirit. A gentle smile forms upon our lips and our eyes shine with God's Grace and Love and Freedom which becomes the warmth of the shining sun of our open hearts.

This book is pushing you to trust, just for a while, that you are the breath of God, and if you do, then you will become the voice of God yourself.

# CHAPTER 18

# WHO I AM

The statements that I made at the beginning of this book are all the things that I am not. They are all the things that I have experienced through believing my Mind to be who I am. Our Mind creates all those sufferings, all those joys in an uncertain searching for Spirit to reveal itself.

When I live in my Mind and through my Mind and define myself first in my Mind, then all the statements that I made at the beginning of this book are my identity but my Mind is not who I am.

The Rudi I believe I am is a sinner and I am sin. The word sin means 'off centre', 'missed the mark', for when the Mind fires its arrows it sees through blurred duality trying to hit the target of Truth.

My Mind is all my struggling and wrongness and failings identified in judgement. When I live in my Mind I fail, I make mistakes, I am weak and I live a half lived life. I can never get it right ever in my Mind, not ever, because my Mind is not who I am. My Mind is the statements that I made at the beginning of this book but my Mind isn't Rudi.

I am Spirit and my Spirit is Love awakened. My Mind is the suffering dream that creates my drama and story. The real me! I am nothing at all. Rudi is not who I am. All that I have created as Rudi is not who I am.

I am the Spirit and living life of creation that flows through me and when I live as that truth and light I am a servant to God being the same God that lives through me which is all the good that shines out of me when surrendered in God's loving embrace.

I needed to find the truth of Who I am and Why I am here. When you know the truth of Who you are you are not the person that you think you are defined by Mind's story. I had to find that something and to know the Truth, find that one thing I could absolutely trust without doubt and that something is that I am an eternal Spirit of God. Without that I am nothing at all in Mind's dream. I am just a shell feeling empty but when I have absolute faith in knowing that I am this divine Holy Spirit, as you are, then that is where I can always put my trust, my faith and heart.

It will never ever betray me or let me down because this is Who I am, this Love awakened. Everything else that my Mind has created has no true light or glory or joy that is everlasting.

I am not my Mind's personality. When I live as my Spirit within me I am forgiven and released of all my sins and Mind's controls. I am not the Me Mind. I am the love and the light and the truth and so are you. Knowing it is redemption, it heals me and it fills me with the light of God so I can become a light of God, an ambassador for truth, freedom and love.

I am nothing but a servant of my father which is God. I am a servant of the most high and glorious force of the universe for I am that living force and in that is all redemption and all life and all knowing.

It is not about Rudi and what I need or want or desire. It is not about what I should have or should do to become this powerful Mind person for I am nothing without the Holy Spirit living through me. I am nothing at all but when I am the silence and the peace within me I am everything to the world which cannot be defined through persona.

We are all living lights and the truth of God. That is what we must begin our day knowing and end our day knowing. Anything else and you become a servant of the Mind. God lives in me and I live in God's glory, power and strength for I am of that.

Life is full when the God that you are lives through you. With that power then you can overcome anything, any obstacle, without fear and without uncertainty. It is a power beyond Mind's imagination.

### I AM ALIVE FOREVER

### I WAS NEVER BORN AND CAN NEVER DIE.

### FOR I AM THE LIVING LONGING OF LOVE!

### I'M THE IT!

### THAT'S WHO I AM

It is only through surrendering absolutely to this Oneness within you with absolute trust and conviction that you are freed of all sin and become the light that gives permission for everyone around you to become their Holy Spirit.

Through your light you give others the opportunity to truthfully shine in their own light. If you are a Spirit of God awakened then there are no words, only the shining example of your presence that reminds people of who they are, so they too can shine from the heart of Love and each become lights to the world.

This will wipe away all Mind's suffering and wrong doing where humankind can reveal its true purpose on this planet, called Earth, our Garden of Eden among the stars.

I AM

as you are

LOVE AWAKENED IN MIND'S DREAM.

WITHOUT THE MIND'S DREAM

WE ARE LOVE.

There is nothing else.

# NOTES

## CHAPTER 1 THE CALLING

Page 7 *'Conversations with God' by Neale Donald Walsch.*

## CHAPTER 5 ASCENSION

Page 68 Matthew 17:20 The Bible New International Version (1984)'

## CHAPTER 8 LOVE & RELATIONSHIPS

Page 116 *'Men are from Mars, Women are from Venus' by John Gray.*

## CHAPTER 9 THEATRE OF THE MIND

Page 139 'As You Like it' William Shakespeare

Page 139 'As A Man Thinketh' (1902) by James Allen

## CHAPTER 10 – THE GOD OF JUDGEMENT

Page 175 Mark 12:31 The Bible New Living Translation (2007)

Page 175 John 20:21 The Bible New Living Translation (2007)

## CHAPTER 13 THE FEELING UNIVERSE

Page 215 Luke 9:58 King James 2000 Bible (2003)

## CHAPTER 14 LIFE FORCE

Page 252 Matthew 21:12 'And Jesus *went into the temple of God, and cast out all them that sold and bought in the temple, and overthrew the tables of the money changers, and the seats of them that sold doves.' King James 2000 Bible (2003)*

## ABOUT THE AUTHOR

Rudi is a prolific speaker on the Eternal Spirit, sharing his understanding of the human condition which he has learnt from many thousands of one to one intuitive Spiritual consultations.

He runs regular courses and workshops inspiring people to find out who they are. He shares his Soul journey through his unique personality that has made him an inspirational speaker in many venues including TV and radio. He has the gift to uplift and motivate people to live their life in love, peace and freedom.

Rudi has studied and practised many systems of Eastern and Western holistic and Spiritual wisdom. He has an ability to bring in and piece together new parts of the jigsaw of human experience helping us see the bigger picture, for we all need to place our own individual special shining pieces into God's picture of Love.

For information about his workshops and courses go to his website **www.clairvoyant.co.uk**

Printed in Great Britain
by Amazon

14261913R00190